The Life of the African-American Career Military Woman: An Autoethnographic Study

Camelia Straughn, DBA

Table of Contents

AUTHORS' BIOGRAPHIES……………………..3

ACKNOWLEDGEMENTS…………………….....4

INTRODUCTION…………………………………6

SECTION I: FUNDAMENTAL ELEMENTS…13

Chapter 1: The Organizational, Social, and Personal Challenges for the African-American Career Military Woman in Military Culture……………………..14

Chapter 2: Theoretical and Conceptual Framework…………………………………………..21

Chapter 3: African-American Women and the Military……………………………………………39

SECTION II: AUTOETHNOGRAPHY…………54

Chapter 4: Research Methodology……………….55

Chapter 5: Findings……………………………….78

Chapter 6: The Autoethnography…………………85

Chapter 7: Discussion and Implications………..128

Chapter 8: Recommendations and Conclusions..139

Bibliography……………………………………..147

AUTHOR'S BIOGRAPHY

Camelia Straughn, DBA is the oldest child born to her mother and her father. At the age of 5 she was raped by her youngest sister's uncle. At the age of 12 her mother's boyfriend sexually assaulted her. Then from the age of 13-17 she was forced into a sexual relationship with two of her uncles. So, at the age of 18 she got married, after the "I do's" she quickly learned that her husband would make it a weekly tradition to beat her. She stayed for 3 years. She is also a survivor of Military sexual trauma. For years she struggled with the thought that she was not enough. This way of thinking affected how she showed up in the world. She knew she did not want to continue to live her life in such depression and a life cycle of feast to famine. Through her passion for sexual assault/domestic violence victims/survivors and self-esteem building, she was able to move from the idea of not being enough to knowing that SHE IS Enough! Dr. Straughn has dedicated her life to teaching others the same.

Dr. Straughn is also a 23-year Retired Army veteran, with more than half of which she spent training & counseling soldiers. A doctorate in Organizational Leadership & Behavior. A BS & MBA specializing in

Human Resources. A life story of trial & absolute triumph.

Dr. Straughn founded RisingSTAR Coaching to disrupt the way women view themselves, heal their hearts and create a life of BLISS. She has been helping women and men transform their lives since 2009. She is the author of 4 books with the most recent one being "Finding Your BLISS in the Midst of Pain: 9 Keys to Trusting Yourself and Living an Extraordinary Life". She is a motivational speaker, Life-Career Transformational Coach, Mentor and Author.

ACKNOWLEDGEMENTS

I have to start with thanking my Mother, Diane D. Williams (January 21, 1951 – October 4, 2004), who at 17 made the decision to give birth to me, despite circumstances and living in Alabama during the late 60's (1968 to be exact). I will forever love you for giving me a chance to live.

I want to also thank my children: Timethius, Jacarah and Jawara. Thank you for saying yes to Sprit when given the option to enter this physical plain through. Thank you for stretching me and believing in me as a Mother and loving me in my mistakes as I worked to learn how to be the best mother for you all as a collective and as individuals. To Sabrina who is just like a daughter to me, thank you for blessing me with my beautiful granddaughter Temani. Thank you for allowing me to continue to be a part of yours and Temani's life. You all are my WHY! ~Love Mommy!

Next, I want to thank my Mentor Dr. Daphne Halkias for her continued support, for assisting me with standing in my truth when working on my dissertation which this book is a byproduct of! Thank you for writing the introduction and encouraging me to write this book.

Finally, and most importantly, I want to thank the Creator for guiding and giving me the strength, wisdom and courage that helped me to endure all the hurt, abuse, trauma and disappointment, which helped me to move from Broken to Brilliant.

INTRODUCTION

A Woman of Courage and Strength tells her Story

Daphne Halkias, PhD.
International School of Management
Paris, France

When I first met Dr. Camelia Straughn she was my doctoral student: a 46-year old career military African-American woman, a Sergeant First Class serving at the 185th MP BN (Military police Battalion) in Pittsburgh, California. During her doctoral studies Camelia also served as Vulnerability Non-Commissioned Officer (NCO), Physical Security NCO, Sexual Assault Advocate, Safety NCO, and Equal Employment Opportunity NCO. The subject has also served as a Platoon Sergeant for the 270th MP co during their deployment to Guantanamo Bay, Cuba. She was living with her three children in Sacramento, California and simultaneously works in a second career as a Career/Life Coach and Beauty Consultant while also completing her doctoral studies. Over the course of completing her doctoral studies, Camelia faced many financial and family challenges. Yet, through it all, including a stint of homelessness and living in a motel with her children, she never let up on writing her doctoral dissertation. This woman had my respect and admiration is someone I easily see as role model not just for African- American women, but women everywhere working and raising their children while also contributing to community through her service and support.

Conducting life history and autoethnographic research as Camelia has done here in her book, allows narrators as her to contribute to set the agenda for further research in their field of critical race and feminist literature. Autoethnography is ethnographic in its methodological orientation and uses the autobiographic materials of the researcher as the primary data emphasizing cultural analysis and interpretation of the researcher's behaviors, thoughts, and experiences in relation to others in society. The life story interview based on the Labovian approach guided the qualitative autoethnography during the exploration of self-observations and stories. The Labovian approach requires the researcher to answer questions, where she is both the interviewee and the interviewer. Via the life history process, a narrative is constructed so as to make sense of the narration; bringing the storyteller's meanings and interpretations to the reader.

Examining the daily life of the African-American career military woman through the first-person narrative and emergent themes of autoethnography will contribute valuable insight to the integration of race, gender, and military scholarly literature. The information disseminated from this study may help leaders' efficacy in leading, training and supporting the African-American career military woman. This information may also help leaders choose African-American women as leaders based on their individual merit and not based on stereotypes. Stereotypes can affect African- American women in leadership roles because of their influence on perceptions and their elicitation of stereotype threat. Camelia's story is also a study in intersectionality. Scholars agree that a lack of understanding of the intersectionality of minorities, especially African-American women, exists in the organizational leadership literature.

A personal narrative is a creative way for a writer to share some life experiences with their readers. A personal narrative tells a story and lets the reader become part of the storyteller's life. Camelia's personal narratives is important in that it brought to light the challenges that were unique and specific to the African-American career military woman on the integration of military culture, gender and race for women of color. In doing this it allowed for others to understand and begin to discuss these challenges, which in turn creates an environment that allowed for the African-American career military woman to be seen and treated as a viable part of the military. This study provided an in-depth look and gave a vice to the African-American career military women who hold leadership roles and who also encounter organizational and social barriers in the military due to their race and gender. The information disseminated from this study might help leaders' efficacy in leading, training and supporting the African-American career military woman. Scholars agree that a lack of understanding of the intersectionality of minorities, especially African-American women, exists in the organizational leadership literature. In order to begin that undertaking, a clear understanding of the interconnected effects of race, economic conditions, and gender within the military was evaluated through research founded on qualitative narratives as in Camelia's story in this book.

Camelia's literature review in her book directs its focus on exploring previous and current literature that will address the issues related to the African-American career woman as she works to balance and successfully integrate military life, gender, and race. To support this autoethnography study, Camelia used the theoretical framework of Derrick Bell's (1995) CRT in relation to African-American women, leadership, and the concept of intersectionality (Parker, 2001). To establish a theoretical base for the study, articles from peer-reviewed journals will be searched and reviewed. This exercise will help to also gather information on the study's methods and historical background.

For a long time, race has been a social justice issue in the United States, and within this context individuals have had to struggle for success solely on the basis of merit. African-American women are faced with discrimination in relation to both gender and race, largely as a result of their marginalization in the US workplace. Historically, Black women have been central figures in the fight for human and civil rights, driven by a desire to sustain families and communities, and laying the foundation of the unique character of the US as a nation (Rosser-Mims, 2010). The challenges experienced by African-

American women in many organizations have led to barriers that severely affect their chances of being selected for leadership positions at the highest organizational levels. A study by Cook and Glass (2016) found that many organizations — including as the military — do not recruit for or hire Black women for leadership positions merely on account of their race and gender.

These authors further noted that, more often than not, there is a belief that African-American women do not possess the skills and competencies required to successfully lead an organization. In the same vein, other research underlines that Black women have to deal with marginalization and discrimination on account of them being deemed unqualified for leadership positions in the workplace due to their race and gender status and the perception that they are inferior to their White counterparts (Emerson & Murphy, 2014). Further, the fact of their gender and race mean they are often overlooked for leadership positions as African-American women do not exemplify the characteristics typically associated with a leader (Livingston, Rosette, & Washington, 2012).

Camelia's story will show and evidence the crucial role that African-American women have played in every US war effort. They have had to deal with both criticism at a personal level and challenges to their physical capabilities, all the while with many of their contributions going unrewarded and even unrecognized.

These astounding women have endured lives fraught with dangers while giving of their abilities and strengths in order to secure freedom and uphold values. Several million men and women of color currently wear the uniform of the US military. An ever-richer and more voluminous body of literature delves into the experiences of African-Americans in the military, both at the individual and community level.

This book is Camelia's story and it could be the story of many women. Throughout her whole life and even as a career military African-American woman, Camelia found herself as part of marginalized groups of those who face daily challenges through the lens of gender, race and culture. Research on organizations, such as the military, has used many theoretical and exploratory perspectives to understand differences in "diversity" or marginalized groups. The life of the African- American career military woman is often dominated by the organizational, social and personal challenges that she will encounter as a woman of color. Exploring her life story, Camelia offers us a view of daily life, first of an African-American young girl and then, as a professional woman. Camelia's story helps us gain valuable insight into a courageous life lived at the crossroads of race, gender, family and work life.

SECTION I: FUNDAMENTAL ELEMENTS

Chapter 1

The Organizational, Social, and Personal Challenges for the African-American Career Military Woman in Military Culture

Half of the women serving in the military are minority women, with African-Americans accounting for 30% of all military women. The demographic data that were collected by the U.S. Department of Defense in a 2013 summary report revealed that while African-American women represented 31% of the 167,000 enlisted military women, this number was twice that percentage in the U.S. civilian population. Although white women make up 53% of women in the military at this time, this representation is considerably low given their civilian composition of 78%. Furthermore, the enlistment rate of African-American women is even higher than that of African-American men, whose military representation is roughly equal to their proportion in the civilian population.

For many young African-American women, joining the military is a transition to an adult military role, rather than a step taken before assuming alternative adult roles. African-American women often face the reality of powerlessness due to the experience of gender and racial oppression that limits, or denies outright, the access to empowering resources such as fair income, education, and employment and positions of prestige and power. Scholars have noted there is a clash between internalized historical representations of the "strong black woman" and social realities that increases the risk of internal distress, feelings of powerlessness, frustration, and anger in African-American women.

Gender as social capital within the military is expressed in assumptions about and direct challenges to women. For example, women have to resort to "pulling rank" more than men to gain compliance from subordinates. Women endure numerous kinds of "tests" (for example, sabotage, constant scrutiny, and indirect threats) that men do not necessarily experience, to prove they are capable of serving in the military. Little is known about the ongoing challenges of career military women since scant literature had been devoted to chronicling their daily lives.

The level on which an African-American career military woman must prove herself as competent and worthy of respect in her professional and personal life, is quite different from both her male and female peers and other males. In studies of incivility due to race and gender, African-American women in the military experienced higher levels of incivility than white women, white men, and African-American men. This social inequality can become more distressing due to the stress overload the African-American military woman experiences throughout her daily life activities. She recognizes that the military is a life of choice and that the benefits of this life outweigh any professional or social inequality she must endure. Yet, in order to be successful as a military career woman, the African-American woman has been called to recognize that she is required to operate in a world with people who at any moment will make it clear to her that she does not belong.

Black women have historically been at the forefront of the struggle for human and civil rights, with the goal of sustaining families and communities, as well as to building the very foundation upon which the United States was built. African-American women can be vocal agents of change within all areas of the African-American communities, the nation through development of their own life narratives. These life stories remain important to accurately represent and interest the range of the African-American woman's diverse experiences. Black women's formal and informal narratives, broad-based oral and intellectual history, and contemporary contributions from all walks of life have only begun to gain due recognition.

In exploring the matrix within which many organizations show the flow of leadership and responsibility one finds that as it relates to holding top leadership roles African-American women continue to be behind the power curve. In that the experiences that African-American women face and how their lives are influenced by intersectional identity African-American women have been singled out due to the intersection of race and gender. Note that the fact and reasoning behind this is grossly under documented. In that there is very little research and documentation because of this, African-American women at best have become known as a marginalized group of women. This in turn has muted

African-American women's voices, leaving their experiences misunderstood and their stories never told.

In order for the intersection of race and gender as it relates to the organizational experiences of African-American women leaders to be fully illustrated, four central ideas are necessary. Those central ideas are the intersectionality of race and gender, diversity and representation of African-American women, devaluation of African-American women within organizations, and the barriers and challenges that are experienced by African-American women within organizations.

The enlistment of African-American women in the U.S. military has been a persistent and growing demographic trend with black women now making up over one third of all women in the U.S. military. Regarding the role of African-American women in the American military, AAWs have played a vital role in every war effort in United States history. The African-American woman endured physical discomfort and personal criticism, while many of their contributions were unrecognized and unrewarded. In the wake of all the dangers that they faced during American wars, African-American women also faced gendered and racial discrimination as part of their military service. Through the progression of the years and the wars, the duties and responsibilities of the African-American woman who became a soldier went from domestic duties to leading troops. In 1994, the Army dropped a rule prohibiting women from filling positions with a "substantial risk of capture". These changes opened up 90% of military jobs to women for the first time. Today women "openly" take infantry training alongside men. They work as engineers, truck drivers, pilots, and weapons experts. A total of 16% of female officers and 34% of enlisted women are black compared with 9% of male officers and 20% of enlisted men. In the Army, close to one-fourth of women officers and nearly one-half of enlisted women are black. In addition, black women are better represented than white women among noncommissioned officers, which reflects their longer stay in the service.

Yet, research has also revealed that, though progress continues, racial friction is still a pressing problem and prejudices based on race and gender, remain a serious obstacle to the military's goal of racial neutrality. Researchers have cited that such racial incidents reported by both African-Americans and Latinos have caused minority military personnel to lose trust in their fellow soldiers, undermining efforts to work effectively together. Because gender stereotypes are not uniform across all racial groups, the experiences of minority women have been and continue to be attributed to interactions between race and gender. Researchers in a variety of disciplines including sociology, demography, economics, and management refer to this interaction as "double jeopardy". In light of these realities and statistics, African-American women usually choose to focus on the benefits of being in the military and coping in various ways with sexual discrimination and harassment as it arises. For the African-American woman a key element to maintaining her military status has become learning how to deal with traumatic personal experiences such as racial discrimination, sexual harassment and gender discrimination while not allowing the problem to get in the way of her success or the success of her family.

The problem is that the life of the African-American career military woman, a member of a marginalized population group, is often dominated by the organizational, social and personal challenges that she will encounter as a woman of color in military culture. New types of questions about women's lives in marginalized population groups need to be addressed within their respective fields of research, including the cross-disciplinary field of gender, race and military science. Research on organizations, such as the military, has used many theoretical and research perspectives to understand differences in "diversity" or marginalized groups. However, little is known about the mechanisms that perpetuate and sustain those differences and scholars have not appreciated the use of the word "diversity" as it obscures the reason for examining marginalized groups and avoids issues of prejudice and discrimination diversity programs may fail to interrupt, or challenge.

Feminist scholars have developed a large literature on women in militaries, and they recognize the military is an important site for the socially dominant ideas about gender. However, very little of this work examines the integration of military life, gender, and race in the daily lives of the African-American woman. The chronic gap in literature on the integration of military life, gender, and race in the daily life of the African-American woman can possibly lead to mentors, counselors, and military policy makers having little insight into the unique daily stressors faced by an African-American woman who has made the military her career profession.

Chapter 2

Theoretical and Conceptual Framework

The theoretical framework that was used to support this autoethnography study is that of Derrick Bell's (1995) critical race theory (CRT) as it pertains to African-American women, leadership and the concept of intersectionality. CRT is based on the idea of social construction. Social construct is defined as an idea, connotation or notion of creating social reality. For this project, we will look at the maintenance of the socially constructed categories of race and gender. Looking at the reality of race and that racism is a disease that is a permanent part of society and intersects with other forms of oppression such as class discrimination, gender, ethnic and sexual minority oppression. The CRT framework imparts a complete view of the marginalization of African-American women via discrimination and racism. Due to the negative racial awareness that is so enmeshed in the fabric of the United States' social order, CRT considers the social construction of race and racism as long-lasting features of American society. The fact that racism and racist acts have gone unchecked, appears to be normal and natural to many people, which causes it to be unrecognized as well. Because CRT has roots in legal studies and its concept to understanding race and African-American women as it pertains to their experiences of gender and race, as they try to maneuver through organizations, CRT has become the main theory used and studied to assist with and focus on telling the African-American woman's story.

The CRT theory is used in research of studies involving African-American faculty members when it came to addressing the challenges they faced concerning academia tenure, based on their race. In 2012, Garrison-Wade, Diggs, Estrada, and Galindo used CRT as the theoretical foundation for their research to show that higher education institutions did not value the concept of having diversity within the institution as it relates to faculty who were African-American. This concept of having academia faculty of color was a challenge mainly due to White America not seeing the benefits of incorporating a diverse model within the higher education institutions. Additionally, the use of CRT focused on and gave clear details of the social injustices imparted upon minorities. This research mirrors with that of Garrison et al. (2012) in that it gives focus to the social injustice African-American women experience in organizations also in the way CRT is used by the author. Being that White American does not value the worth, potential, nor do they see the need for diversity within the higher education institutions, this concept and way of doing business also becomes a part of the culture of organizations outside of the education realm. CRT emphasized and illustrated the limitations of social justice for minorities where there was a lack of diversity in leadership roles. This research study coincides with Garrison et al. (2012) because it focuses on the social injustice that African-American women encounter in the workplace and the way in which the authors used CRT.

When it comes to understanding African-American women and their plight to move past the institutional barriers that play a great part in limiting their advancement within organizations, CRT helps in this case. CRT also assists with the process of making clear and aligning intersectionality as the reason for the current lack and the future of African-American women moving into leadership roles within organizations. Furthermore, according to Rocco, Bernier, and Bowman (2014) CRT is a tool that one can use to help others to understand the social structures that dominate and oppress a group of people. This is so because a lack of diversity within an organization due to the leadership not mirroring the demographics of the entire workforce limits appropriate mentorship opportunities for minorities, which can hinder an organization's workforce productivity, CRT promotes the idea of taking a critical look at this issue. With reference to this research study, African-American women, their experiences of oppression, and the barriers that exist due to race and gender CRT provides a foundation for further investigation into organizations.

In terms of race and gender, one of the six tenets of CRT is intersectionality. Intersectionality highlights different ways in which African-American women have experienced oppression due to their race and gender. The central hypothesis of the intersectionality concept is to discover the magnitude of how race and gender affect the lived experiences encountered on a day-to-day basis by African-American women in leadership roles. Parker's

(2005) description included intersectionality as a tool for analyzing and creating a clear illustration of the experiences that African-American women endure while holding leadership positions within predominantly White organizations. By using an analytical approach, intersectionality is providing the meaning and consequences of multiple categories of social group membership. When exploring leadership in the workplace the concept of intersectionality is especially suitable because it provides an understanding of the connection between multiple social factors and multiple identities and how those factors and identities shape leadership effectiveness, identity, and behavior.

The concept of the intersectionality of race and gender is critical to the foundation of this research study. Intersectionality conceptualizes and has also been applied to understand racism, sexism, and other forms of bigotry that create several barriers that prevent a minority woman's rise to a high-powered, high-level political position. Sanchez-Hucles and Davis (2010) asserted that cross-cultural psychologists have applied the intersectionality of race and gender to study the socialization in several different cultures to understand identity and social interaction formation. The intersectionality of race and gender has been utilized across many different types of industries and many different studies. It is a concept that works to promote an understanding of why a specific group of people encounters barriers; it is used to challenge the inequality of a group of people, and finally, it is used to understand why a certain group of people are marginalized, and not given the opportunity to attain a higher level of success.

The research questions of this study relate to the intersectionality of race and gender concept because it focuses the attention on a group of people who have been denied a higher level of success within an organization and who have experienced race gender segregation due to their race and gender. According to Powell (2012), in recent years the representation of African-American women is thinly dispersed at best and the number of women who hold leadership positions within corporate offices, boardrooms, and executive suites have plateaued. Intersectionality makes the difference between the barriers African-American women encounter and the strategies that they have used to overcome those barriers and find success smaller.

As noted by Wilton, Good, Moss-Racusin, and Sanchez (2014), there is experimental and field evidence documenting the ever-present existence of discrimination of both race and gender prejudice. These prejudices negatively affect the promotional potential of African-American women within the workplace. Furthermore, the intersectionality of race and gender concept will help to answer questions regarding African-American women and how their identity, and the perceptions of them, contributes to their leadership experiences. In addition, intersectionality plays a significant role in creating a complete picture of the career path and trajectory of African-American women within organizations due to its focus on race and gender and how race and gender determine the professional climb up the corporate ladder within organizations.

Demographics and Census Data on African-American Women in the Workplace

African-American women experience gender and race discrimination, which is largely due to them being marginalized in the American workplace. Due to the racial and gender discrimination that African-American women in the workplace experience, frequent exclusions are brought about from leadership development and promotion opportunities within the organizations they work in. Statistics show that African-American women represent 6.4% of the population, but they only hold 2% of mathematics and science jobs and 2.4% of science and engineering jobs. When researching the 2013 Catalyst census on women in corporate leadership positions within the 471 Fortune 500 companies, African-American women only hold 172 or 3.2% of the 5,306 directorship positions that were available within corporate America. According to the results of a survey done by the Catalyst (2013) for the 471 Fortune 500 companies, 318 companies reported no women of color as corporate officers, 134 reported one, 19 reported two, but none of the companies surveyed had three or more women of color occupying corporate leadership positions (p. 2). Warner (2014) corroborated the statistical data provided by Catalyst (2013) in where they stated that women of color represent 36.3% of the nation's female population, yet they only hold 11.9% of the managerial and professional positions, with African-

American women holding only 5.3% of those managerial and professional positions.

Women of color make up only 4.5% of the 113th Congress. When looking at the representation of women of color at the State level the representation is even lower, showing that only 5% of the state legislators are represented by women of color, moreover they represent only 20.8% of female state legislators and 3.5% of governors. When looking at statistics from 2002 African-American women were found to have held only 106 of the 10,092 corporate office positions, or one could say they held a miniscule percentage of 1.1% of those corporate positions.

The wage gaps between African-American women and other races raise a question about economic security. The question of economic security came to clear light in 2013, when white women experienced a 29% inflation adjusted income increase where the wage increase for African-American women was significantly lower at 19% according to Catalyst (2013, p. 1). The U.S. Bureau of Labor Statistics (2014) confirmed these numbers by stating that growth earnings were at its greatest for White women and they were out pacing their Black counter parts. The predictor of potential earning in this study was historical data; this data suggested that regardless of their skills, qualifications or inherent potential, African-American women most likely will continue to lag behind their Caucasian counterparts. Ahmad and Iverson (2013) stated that in 2010 white women made 78.1 cents to the dollar, whereas African-

American women made 64 cents to the same dollar. The examination of African-American women who have risen to leadership positions brings to conclusion that their voices have been "muted, obscured, or not mentioned" and they are absent from mainstream leadership literature.

The African-American woman's unique history, which dates back to slavery, has greatly influenced the wages they bring home and the relationships that they have with their organizational affiliates. Catalyst (2004) states that the separation and preference of light-skinned more European looking Black women over darker skin Black women began with slavery. It is argued that this separation and preferential treatment is prevalent today where light-skinned and more European in appearance black women are happier and more satisfied with their opportunities of advancements as well as their wages than black women who are of darker skin complexion. The Bureau of Labor Statistics (2014) reviewed the income levels of African-American women compared to their white counterparts and found an 84% difference in their weekly wages. Simply put, the black woman earned $599 on a weekly basis while white women earned approximately $710 on a weekly basis. The disparities that African-American women continue to encounter creates a world where they are consistently earning less than their white counter parts and they are not given the opportunities to obtain top leadership roles and experiences. Furthermore, these disparities continue to be absent from mainstream research and this absence continues to mute the voices of African-American women.

Themes in the Lives of African-American Women in America Today
Black women have historically been at the forefront of the struggle for human and civil rights, with the goal of sustaining families, communities, and to building the very foundation upon which the United States is built. African-American women can be vocal agents of change within all areas of the African-American communities, the nation, and the Diaspora through development of their own life narratives. These life stories remain important to accurately represent and interest the range of the African-American woman's diverse experiences. Black women's formal and informal narratives, broad-based oral and intellectual history, and contemporary contributions from all walks of life have only begun to gain due recognition. Self-concept is a multi-dimensional construct that refers to an individual's perception of "self" in relation to any number of characteristics. Self-concept for the African-American woman is generally positive. Historically, social scientists posited negative psychological outcomes for African-Americans. It was generally thought that an environment of racial oppression and segregation would devastate the black psyche and cause self-hatred and low self-esteem. From the beginning of life black girls are socialized differently than white girls—a relic of slavery and, later, employment discrimination. Slave women had to be self-reliant and self-sufficient to develop their own means of survival because black men were often not

present to take care of them and their families. Slave women also relied on each other in what whites called: "female slave network." They helped each other in the field, with household duties, and with the care of children.

This self-reliant and self-sufficient way of thinking is still prevalent in the African-American community among African-American women even today. It is important to look at the "strong woman syndrome" that African-American women continue to struggle with, working to unpack sexism and racism in the black community, and addressing the challenges that black women face on daily basis in society. For the African-American woman of today it can be said that she holds a unique position in this country. She is "confronted by both a woman question and a race problem" (Rosser-Mims, 2010, p. 2).
Some authors have suggested that cultural expectation of strength in African-American women fuels the myth of the "strong black woman" that compels the woman to push for unrealistic levels of self-sacrifice, self-denial and ensuing emotional distress. It is this combination of "powerlessness" and "strength" that presents a problematic paradox for African-American women, finding themselves at the highest risk of internalizing a sense of powerlessness as the result of experiencing gender and racial oppression. At the same time, these social conditions have contributed to the disproportionate representation of African-American women at the bottom of the income, education, and

employment categories and at the top of the poverty levels.

The Intersectional Identity of African-American Women

Race, even when paired with ethnicity, encapsulates multiple social realities always inflected through gender and class differences. 'Class' is also complicated by multiple gendered and racialized differences. The conclusion to this line of thinking—theory and research on inequality, dominance, and oppression must pay attention to the intersections of, at least, race/ethnicity, gender, and class.

In 1980, a discussion and focus on the black woman's experience as it pertains to intersectionality began to surface and became a topic of interest. A discussion was then fostered around a new view of the experience of social identity, due to the new perspective on the lived experiences of oppression that African-American woman encountered based on the role that race and gender played via those encounters. The emergence of intersectionality became a major paradigm in women's studies, yet, along with the emergence, how to study it has not been widely discussed; the reality is that a methodology has not been identified or practiced that would assist in adequately studying intersectionality. This has created great concern regarding how the concept of intersectionality has been studied and taken up.

Arifeen and Gatrell (2013) suggest using a methodological approach that views identity as a process when researching the role of intersectionality identity in women and consider qualitative methods particularly useful because "qualitative methodological approach pays particular attention to subjective experience, and how this experience is dependent on one's social location" (Warner, 2008). Bowleg (2008) further supports qualitative methodology in stating that "...intersectionality cannot be expressed mathematically in a formula nor can it be a layered-on-approach as in a multi layered cake or pyramid" (p. 7). Simply put, mathematical equations and statistics do not account for the experiences, the stories or the voices of African-American women, so it would not be useful to study intersectionality in that manner. Warner (2008) further supports Bowleg (2008) by insisting that qualitative methods do not depend on *a priori* hypothesis, instead the stories and experiences of the respondents, creating an unexpected outcome from groups that are marginalized and underrepresented in theory.

The African-American woman's epistemology is rooted in the affluence of their African heritage that imparts what they believe to be authentic about themselves and their experiences. In essence, African-American women employ common experiences that occurred historically, such as despotism that began during slavery, and those experiences define their current perspective of how they fit within organizations today. Placing African-American women at the forefront of scholarly analysis creates a precedent from which to study how gender and race intersect with the development of leadership theory within organizations even within the discussion of regulating diversity. Although light has been shed on the many barriers that African-American women encountered in higher education institutions that were predominately white, research lags behind in that most of the women in the study spent their primary and secondary years in the Southern part of the United States when the Civil Rights movement was front and center; i.e., during a time of social and political injustice and mayhem. The other reason the research falls short is that it does not take in to consideration the experiences of the African-American women who did not grow up in the Southern parts but in the Northern parts of the United States. This is important because their lives were not directly impacted by the Civil Rights movement. Therefore, being that these differences were not identified they were also not accounted for; furthermore, the research did not account for the women who grew up after the application of supposed "social justice" that can after the Civil Rights movement this date could show if actual change has happened in experiences that are unique to African-American women. Holvino (2010) stated that, "These processes need to be studied in a double move that breaks them apart and specifies them at the same time that it connects and articulates their relatedness" (p. 262).

One of the barriers that came to light during Remedios and Snyder's (2015) study of the stigmatization of women of color was that there was a lack of tools of measurement to catch the experiences that are unique to multiple-stigmatized targets and it could not effectively put into use what researchers mean by the term intersectionality. The most significant weakness to their review completed by Remedios and Snyder (2015) is their inability to clearly define the term "women of color" when used in their writings. Arifeen and Gatrell (2013) stated that the term "women of color" can embody women who are Black, Pakistani, Asian, Caribbean, etc. Hence, there is no way to decipher which group of women of color Remedios and Snyder (2015) are speaking to, which demonstrates that all women of color are being assigned to one group and not being separated to exhibit true experiences.

Due to the blatant oppression that African-American women encounter, their experiences are very unique to other cultures. As attested by Allen and Butler (2014), black feminist reflection explores the experiences of African-American women as they recount the multiple intersections of despotism along the lines of gender, race and class. The intersections of gender and race are an established reality in the fields of women studies. Nonetheless, just like Remedios and Snyder (2015), Holvino (2010) did not show a contrast in the term "women of color" as speaking to Asian, Latin, Native Americans and Black/African-American women who share a state and reality as racio-ethnic minorities in the United States. This is viewed as one of the major drawbacks in the most current literature pertaining to the intersectionality of gender and race for African-American women. The unique experiences of African-American women were studied in the grand scheme of "women of color" instead of being detached and studied as an individual unit. Jean-Marie, Williams, and Sherman (2009) asserted that the experiences of black women have been removed, marginalized, and distorted, rendering their voices muted and them as a group obliterated.

The Challenges of Attaining Leadership Positions for African-American Women

Barriers that are created via the challenges that African-American women experience within many organizations make it less likely that they will be chosen for leadership positions that fall within the top tier of the organization matrix. Cook and Glass (2013) stated that many organizations do not assign African-American women to leadership positions simply because they are black and women. They also asserted that it is most often than not, believed that they do not have the necessary capabilities to lead organizations. Additionally, the authors asserted that minority women when compared to their White counterparts are viewed as less capable of leading organizations by those people who are deemed as the decision makers. Emerson and Murphy (2014) stated that because of their race and gender African-American women are perceived as inferior to their white counterparts, in turn they face the challenges of marginalization and discrimination in that they are not considered "qualified" for leadership positions in the workplace. Rosette and Livingston (2012) suggested that because African-American women do not meet the typical characteristics of a leader, they suffer because of their gender and race and are not considered for leadership positions.

According to Lloyd-Jones (2014), African-American women are socially and scholarly marginalized, which serves as a barrier to African-American women being promoted, and it creates barriers with obtaining tenure in higher education institutions. Isolation becomes a challenge for the African-American woman, because she is not given the opportunities to succeed or become a leader. The reason for this is that she is simply not exposed to the tasks that would assist her in being promoted. The high visibility challenge as explained by Cook and Glass (2013) is when an organization "keeps an eye on" the African-American woman. The high visibility challenge is put in place to ensure that the African-American woman who is put in a middle-management leadership position is completing the tasks given to her, while ensuring that she is not exposed to tasks that would create opportunities of advancement into top leadership positions. Additionally, another challenge that is prevalent within organizations where African-American women are the main target, is gender harassment. According to Johnson and Thomas (2012), selective incivility creates barriers as well as challenges for African-American women in being promoted within organizations. The reasoning behind this is that organizations see African-American women as belonging to a group that is socially undervalued. This belief makes it nearly impossible for African-American women to acquire positions of leadership.

Being that diversity within organizations is aimed at an inclusive work environment for all employees makes it an important topic within organizations. Diversity within organizations emphasizes the understanding and importance of the inclusion of different types of people in a group or organization. This understanding will reduce or eliminate discrimination in the workplace. Ferdman and Sagiv (2012) also stated that the benefit of understanding diversity is that it will maximize the inclusion and contributions of individuals, increase equality as well as social justice along with creating greater organizational success. When it comes to the dynamics of an organization, race is an important factor. The diversity factor as it pertains to African-American women is still lacking, even though it is incorporated in organizations under the auspiciousness of inclusion, social justice, and equality. However, Festekjian, Tram, Murray, Sy, and Huynh (2014) stated there is still a lack of minority representation, even though organizations have called for diversity to be implemented within organizations.

When addressing the experiences of women of color when they were working within predominantly white universities, Turner, Gonzalez, and Lau (2011) focused on looking at specifically the experiences of African-American women, which showed a decrease in women of color within professional ranks, which in turn resulted in underrepresentation of African-American women. When looking at the workforce as it pertains to managerial and professional positions research shows that only 12 of this particular group are women of color.

Research also shows that for Fortune 500 companies only 3% of the directors are women of color and only three women of color hold the position of Chief Executive Officer (CEO). What these numbers show is that equal representation and the call for diversification has essentially been unsuccessful within organizations in regard to African-American women. Due to her race and gender not aligning with that of the prototypical leader, organizations continue to mask opportunities for the advancement of the African-American woman and continue to deem African-American women as not being capable of leading and being intellectually and morally inferior.

Chapter 3

African-American Women and the Military

A Brief History
African-American women have played a vital role in every war effort in United States history. The African-American woman endured physical discomfort and personal criticism, while many of their contributions were unrecognized and unrewarded. These amazing women placed themselves in danger's path—offering their strengths and abilities to preserve values and ensure freedom. They stood side by side with fathers, husbands, and sons to nurse and comfort the suffering; they engaged in the danger of spying, chronicled the pain of war, and offered spiritual healing. In the wake of all the dangers that they faced during the war African-American women also faced gender and racial discrimination as part of their military service. These pioneering women simultaneously mastered the art of building and sustaining family and community life while dealing with wars. African-American women have always been active participants in the military. They were always there!

African-American women participated in the Revolutionary War (1775–1783) and the War of 1812. These women kept the colonial authorities informed about the British activities by serving as spies during the Revolutionary War. According to written accounts by Lucy Terry, African-American women disguised themselves as men and fought side by side with them against the British. During the War of 1812, their role of service was limited to making bandages and taking care of sick and wounded soldiers. They also worked the farms that belonged to the white male Soldiers so they could go to war knowing that their lands, animals, and produce were in good hands.

The Civil War took place from 1861–1865 and during this time African-American women served as nurses, completed domestic chores in medical settings, laundering and cooking for the soldiers. African-American women were paid by the Union Army to raise cotton for the northern government to sell. In 1902, when Harriet Tubman's memoirs were published, they become the only written record of black volunteer nurses in the Civil War. Susan Taylor King, a former slave who was raised on an island off the coast of Georgia, became famous while serving during the Civil War as a volunteer. King's experiences are recounted in her diary as she wrote of unequal treatment:

> The first colored troops did not receive any pay for 18 months and the men had to depend wholly on what they received from the commissary...their wives were obliged to support themselves and children by washing for the officers and making cakes and pies which they sold to the boys in the camp. Finally, in 1863, the government decided to give them half pay, but the men would accept none of this. They preferred rather to give their services to the state, which they did until 1964, when the government granted them full pay, with all back due pay. (Taylor, 1988 p. 154)

Susan King served for four years and three months and was never paid for her service. African-American women served in the Spanish American War (1898), World War I (1914–1918), World War II (1939–1945), Korean War (1950–1953), Viet Nam (1959–1975), The Persian Gulf War (1990–1991) and the War in Iraq and Afghanistan (2003–current). Through the progression of the years and the wars, the duties and responsibilities of the African-American woman who became a soldier went from domestic duties to leading troops. In 1994, the Army dropped a rule prohibiting women from filing positions with a "substantial risk of capture". These changes opened up 90% of military jobs to women for the first time. Today women "openly" take infantry training alongside men. They work as engineers, truck drivers, pilots, and weapons experts. According to a 2005 report, African-American women see the military as providing greater opportunities and benefits than the civilian labor market. A total of 16% of female officers and 34% of enlisted women are black compared with 9% of male officers and 20% of enlisted men. In the Army, close to one-fourth of women officers and nearly one-half of enlisted women are black. In addition, black women are better represented than white women among noncommissioned officers, which reflects their longer stay in the service.

The Intersection of Race and Gender in Today's Military: The African-American Woman's Perspective

A growing literature explores the military experience of African-Americans as individuals and a community, and while it is always difficult to generalize the experience of a population, the military is largely thought to have played a key social role for the overall community and a positive personal role for individuals. There is also evidence that African-Americans have, for some time, perceived the military as more egalitarian than civilian society, particularly in terms of advancement opportunities and economic stability. Not only has discrimination in the military dramatically abated, but such service also provides an avenue for upward mobility that is not always available in civilian society. The military is still well ahead of the private sector when it comes to incorporating women and minorities into management positions.

Yet, research has also revealed that, though progress continues, racial friction is still a pressing problem and prejudices based on race and gender, remain a serious obstacle to the military's goal of racial neutrality. Researchers have cited that such racial incidents reported by both African-Americans and Latinos have caused minority military personnel to lose trust in their fellow soldiers, undermining efforts to work effectively together. Respondents have also said that nothing was done when the most bothersome episodes were reported to superiors. Despite these difficulties, however, military personnel have repeatedly reported that race relations were better in the military than in the nation as a whole. Because gender stereotypes are not uniform across all racial groups, the experiences of minority women have been and continue to be attributed to interactions between race and gender. Researchers in a variety of disciplines including sociology, demography, economics, and management refer to this interaction as "double jeopardy". Thus, the term "double jeopardy," reflects discrimination as women and as members of racial and/or ethnic minority groups.

Research has shown that sexual harassment is an occupational hazard directly affecting the majority of women across a variety of workplace settings. Depression, posttraumatic stress, and work withdrawal are among a host of individual negative consequences associated with sexual harassment. Sexual harassment refers to a variety of unwanted gender related comments and behaviors, with four subtypes. Gender harassment includes negative verbal and nonverbal behaviors that target an individual based on gender, such as statements that women are less intelligent than men or that they are not fit to do certain types of work. Crude behavior includes offensive verbal and nonverbal sexual behaviors, such as making sexual gestures or jokes. Unwanted sexual attention encompasses unwanted touching or attempts to establish a sexual relationship, including repeatedly asking someone for a date or making attempts to kiss or stroke another person against her will. Lastly, sexual coercion refers to attempts to coerce sexual cooperation via job-related threats or benefits, such as promising a promotion in exchange for sexual activities or threatening to fire someone for refusing to comply with sex-related requests.

Sexual harassment and gender discrimination are both forms of treating women differently and both have been labeled uninvited and unwanted and these constructs remain closely related. In fact, it was suggested that sexual harassment is a form of gender discrimination. Legally, this is the case because sexual harassment is prosecuted as sex discrimination in the United States under Title VII of the Civil Right Act of 1964. However, legal definitions do not always correspond directly to the psychological experience of a phenomenon. Therefore, psychological measures of sexual harassment and gender discrimination may reveal that these constructs function somewhat differently in important and interesting ways.

Sexual harassment and gender discrimination are occupational hazards for the African-American military women in the work place. Among civilians, one-half of working women experience sexual harassment prior to retirement. Rates among military personnel are higher than those for civilian women, with estimates ranging from 65 to 79% of women in the military experiencing sexual harassment within a one-year period upon entering the military. In light of these realities and statistics, African-American women usually choose to focus on the benefits of being in the military and coping in various ways with sexual discrimination and harassment as it arises. For the African-American woman a key element to maintaining her military status has become learning how to deal with traumatic personal experiences such as sexual harassment while not allowing the problem to get in the way of her success or the success of her family.

One characteristic often assigned to military culture is relative race-neutrality. Scholars note that military service may enable African-Americans and Latinos to better succeed in the civilian world. This may be the result of the training received in the military or the post service educational benefits such as the G.I. Bill. The military may also serve as a "bridging environment" that allows minority veterans to better integrate into civilian society (Espino, 2012). One of the few previous studies of this topic, however, showed that African-Americans were no more or less likely than whites to believe there were opportunities for minorities in the military.

The race-friendly environment of the military leads to less racial segregation in housing, education, and socializing. This "race-neutral" environment has been cited by researchers as contributing to lower racial gaps in test scores among military children than in civilian society. Yet, black–white gaps in SAT scores are 30% lower in Department of Defense schools, and gaps in elementary reading and writing test scores are half those found in civilian schools. Educational benefits for African-American women from various forms of the G.I. Bill are a hallmark of the benefits package for those who serve in the armed forces and of the military's aim for racial-neutrality. Other benefits that are available to service members is housing on the military post that they are assigned to and as the times have changed the possibility of advancement has increased for women. Researchers have cited that for the African-American military woman these benefits for themselves and their families far outweigh the trials they face at times of adversity.

Demographics on U.S. Military Families
The U.S. population includes 23.4 million veterans, among them 1.8 million women. In recent decades, the military has downsized by about 30%, but has become busier. Use of the military overseas has tripled. Today, compared to the civilian labor force, members of the active component military force are younger, more ethnically diverse, and better. Military families are about twice as likely as civilian ones to first bear children during their 20s, and less likely to do so in their teens or 30s. Single parents, 70% of them mothers, comprise 5.2% and 8.2% of the active and reserve components, respectively.

Most military families live in civilian communities and most military children attend school in them. Relative to civilians, military families display both strengths and vulnerabilities. Divorce and family formation rates during the all-volunteer era are lower in the active component military than among civilians. Test scores in Department of Defense schools, especially among African-American and Hispanic students, exceed those of most other students around the country. Studies of child abuse have yielded mixed results, but recent studies with larger samples report military rates similar to or lower than those among civilians.

In the United States today, there are several million men and women wearing the uniform of the country's military. In broad terms, this is a young (50% below age 25) and male (85%) population, with individuals from rural, less affluent, and ethnic minority (African-American and Latino/a) backgrounds overrepresented. Almost all have a high school degree or equivalent, and 70% have at least some college credits. About half of them are married, with about 10% of the armed forces in dual-career marriages (i.e., married to another member of the military). In contrast to the U. S. population as a whole, members of the military tend to marry earlier, a fact that researchers need to take into account in comparing military and civilian families because marriage at a younger age can be associated with more problems than marriage at an older age. Among individuals in the armed forces, more than 70% have one or more children, and there are at least 1.85 million children with one or both parents in the military (65% active duty and 35% Reserves or National Guard). Research on military families as well as formal programs to support them often uses a narrow definition of what a family entails: mother and father—one of whom wears a uniform—and their biological children. The so-called nuclear family is not the only type that exists, especially in the contemporary United States. Single-parent families have increased in recent decades, as well as blended families and intergenerational families. With the increase of women in the military, dual-career military families have increased. Each type of family has unique difficulties and assets.

Research on Marriage and Family Life for the African-American Career Military Woman

Race has long tarnished the image of the United States as a context within which individuals can succeed based solely upon merit. After decades of affirmative action and civil rights legislation, Blacks are still less likely than Whites to be fully employed, to be employed in high wage jobs, or to possess important assets such as a house or a retirement program. The military has served as a model for racial integration.

Research has cited that the military service reduces the likelihood of marital dissolution among African-Americans in the Army. The dominating causal factor for this statistic is that the military alters civilian experience of marriage in a fundamental way. This "military culture" alteration allows the effects of norms or culture to be isolated and economic resources are spread much more equitably among service members, minimizing the effects of persistent discrimination that is found in the civilian life that can and does negatively affect marital quality.

Yet, there are opposing interpretations on the state of the military family that delve beyond statistics of marriage and divorce. For example, rates of intimate partner violence, however, are up to three times higher in the military as compared to the civilian population. Intimate partner aggression (IPA) in the military in comparison to civilian rates has yielded some evidence that IPA is more prevalent in active duty than civilian populations.

Some recent studies show that symptoms of combat-related trauma are related to marital distress for both partners. In one study of 45 National Guard couples, wives were more distressed when they could not attribute their husbands' symptoms to an obvious cause, because husbands either failed to acknowledge symptoms the wives perceived or reported more symptoms than their combat experience had led their wives to expect.

After effects of combat wounds and injuries can present families with severe challenges, even when service members fully recover. There are few studies of civilian or military families' process of adjustment to acquired physical injuries. Injuries that cause long-term changes in behavior, emotions, or abilities can seriously challenge marriages. For example, spouses of wounded military personnel are usually placed in care giving, even parental roles, altering or ending their intimate relationship with their partner and increasing their risk of psychological problems and divorce. Military family members may need to relocate or separate to tend to the needs of hospitalized service members during a long rehabilitation. Family members who are not authorized to hold military identification cards face additional challenges because they may have difficulty gaining access to military facilities and services.

So far, recent findings are consistent with earlier research. Among preschoolers, Blais and Boisvert (2005) found elevated internalizing and externalizing behaviors during deployment in a sample of 169 children in child development centers on Marine Corps installations. In a study of 101 Army parents with children age 5 to 12 years and a deployed spouse, 42% reported significant levels of parenting stress and 32% reported significant psychological symptoms in their children. Military parents were seven times more likely to report child symptoms when they also reported high level of stress, but only one third as likely when they felt supported by the military and those around them. A new study of 1,507 children age 11 to 17 and caregivers, found elevated emotional difficulties both during and after deployment, particularly among girls, older children, and children who had experienced longer deployments.

Military families deal with issues common to all families, including child care, elder care, education, parenting concerns, and career choices. The caveat to this that military families are subjected to unique stressors, such as repeated relocations that often include international sites, frequent separations of service members from families, and subsequent reorganizations of family life during reunions. Researchers have cited that perhaps the struggle for the military woman is that both the military and family seek exclusive and undivided loyalty from the member.

In the military culture there is little tolerance for questioning authority. A soldier is constantly prepared for disaster by maintaining physical fitness, training hard, putting the unit before the mission, and never showing weakness. This "culture value" affects the whole family system. Military career women, a demographic group where African-Americans are overrepresented, must always be prepared for disaster whether it is physical disaster, death in a war zone, separation, or relocation. The military career woman must maintain such traits within her family life as secrecy, stoicism, denial of feelings, a heroic stance, strong will-power, identification of action with force, a paranoid worldview, black and white thinking, and often degrading of the feminine.

The average military couple moves every three years but this is more frequent in many cases. This frequent relocation gives a sense that everything is temporary and makes lasting connections difficult. Permanent Change of Station (PCS) may provide an illusion of "escape" for the couple accompanied with hopes that the next assignment will be permanent. The military member is triangulated with his spouse (and family) and the institution of the military. As the family moves through the emotional phases of deployment, the focus of the triangle shifts. In order to reduce the tension associated with this emotional triangle and frequent change of the foci, a member of the triangle may use emotional cutoff as a means to cope with the changes. In light of all of this, the concerns about family issues have become particularly heightened as a result of the increased percentage of women in the military, struggling to balance careers and motherhood. For the African-American woman this is magnified because she is in most cases the sole breadwinner for her family.

With this heightened concern for families, it is particularly important to look at the unique and complex situation of the African-American woman in the military. African-American women have become infamous for always wearing the "strong woman complex," which has hurt them particularly in the realm of mental health and sexual trauma. But, in the military, strength is certainly something that's cultivated and encouraged to be exemplified. Women, in particular, constantly feel the pressure to measure up to their male counterparts, especially in combat zones. African-American women in the military experience another layer of pressure, since many are breadwinners for their families back home as well. African-American women in combat zones continue to experience higher rates of post-traumatic stress disorder (PTSD) due to the assaults that are never reported.

To compound the aforementioned issues there are only 15 Veteran Affairs centers in the United States that provide residential mental-health treatment that is specifically designed for women with PTSD. For those suffering from PTSD, military sexual trauma, or any other mental illness from service, the average wait time for an initial decision for disability benefits and proper treatment is 161 days. These factors have truly made it a struggle for the African-American woman to reintegrate herself back into her civilian life and begin the process to heal from PTSD. Unfortunately, the military women's family can also experience secondary traumatization due to the symptoms of the military spouse/parents, and from hearing the veteran tell stories of the horrific experiences of war. Finally, another issue the military mother must deal with is troubling evidence that child maltreatment rises among military children and within military families during the time the mother is gone on an overseas, training, or combat assignment.

SECTION II: AUTOETHNOGRAPHY

Chapter 4

Research Methodology

The specific problem is that the life of the African-American career military woman, a member of a marginalized population group, is often dominated by the organizational, social and personal challenges that she will encounter as a woman of color in military culture. New types of questions about women's lives in marginalized population groups need to be addressed within their respective fields of research, including the cross-disciplinary field of gender, race and military science. Research on organizations, such as the military, has used many theoretical and research perspectives to understand differences in "diversity" or marginalized groups. However, little is known about the mechanisms that perpetuate and sustain those differences and scholars have not appreciated the use of the word "diversity" as it obscures the reason for examining marginalized groups and avoids issues of prejudice and discrimination diversity programs may fail to interrupt, or challenge.

The purpose of this qualitative study was to explore themes that emerge from the autoethnography of an African-American career military woman on the integration of military culture, gender, and race for women of color. Conducting life history research allows narrators to contribute to setting the agenda for further research in their field of inquiry, in this case military, critical race and feminist literature. Via the life history process, a narrative is constructed bringing the narrator's meanings and interpretations on what the autoethnographic research design.

The research questions developed support the central purpose and methodology of the study. The proposed research problem and purpose of the research has led to two research questions.

Q1: How does an African-American career military woman describe her daily life experiences as defined by race and gender?

Q2: How does an African-American woman describe her daily life experiences as a career military woman through the cultural meanings of her life events, behaviors, and thoughts?

Research Methods and Design
In order to satisfy the purpose of this research, a qualitative autoethnography method was used. Autoethnography is ethnographic in its methodological orientation and uses the autobiographic materials of the researcher as the primary data emphasizing cultural analysis and interpretation of the researcher's behaviors, thoughts, and experiences in relation to others in society. The life story interview based on the Labovian approach guided the qualitative autoethnography during the exploration of self-observations and stories (Labov, 1972, 1982). The Labovian approach requires the researcher to answer questions, where she is both the interviewee and the interviewer. Secondary data collection methods used were common in the autoethnographic methods and which build reflexivity on the collected data: journal records; storytelling of

significant people within the researcher's life; autobiographical writing; historical documents, public records, photographs, and video archival data. Coding and associated categorization of data were conducted using NVivo 10 software. The interweaving of data collection, analysis, and interpretation led to the development of autoethnography. Autoethnography is ethnographic in its methodological orientation and uses the autobiographic materials of the researcher as the primary data emphasizing cultural analysis and interpretation of the researcher's behaviors, thoughts, and experiences in relation to others in society.

Qualitative is a more general and inclusive term that is finding increasing acceptance in the study of such diverse areas as gender, class, and race; and "the complexities of the social world in which we live and how we go about thinking, acting, and making meaning in our lives" (Ellis, 2004, p. 25). To make sense of a life story as research, qualitative techniques and research strategies that include narrative, performative, ethnographic, and autoethnographic, seemed well suited. Autoethnography is an ethnographic inquiry that uses the autobiographic materials of the researcher as the primary data.

Differing from other self-narrative writings such as autobiography and memoir, autoethnography emphasizes cultural analysis and interpretation of the researcher's behaviors, thoughts, and experiences in relation to others in society. This particular qualitative method was developed as women, African-Americans, and other oppressed peoples "insisted that their research projects should make sense in the context of their own lived experiences" (Bochner, 2005, p. 270). For these aforementioned reasons, autoethnography has been chosen as an appropriate method of narrative inquiry for collecting and analyzing the data for this study in order to achieve the research goal of cultural understanding underlying the autobiographical experiences of an African-American career military woman. To achieve this ethnographic intent, the autobiographical materials collected in this study underwent the usual ethnographic research process of data collection, data analysis/interpretation, and report writing.

This study used autoethnography in the form of self-narrative that places the self within the position of an African-American career military woman. The research questions allowed this researcher to speak as a participant/observer from an insider perspective of an African-American career military woman. As an observer, the researcher used introspection in the form of a personal narrative as a primary data source. The rationale for participant observation research was that human behavior is influenced by the context in which it happens. The research paradigm for this study moved between being involved and informed by the researcher's personal experience (interpretive), and an analytic and active learner (critical observer) located in the researcher's interaction within the personal, social, political setting of the life of an African-American career military woman. Therefore, the overarching goal of this inquiry was to interpret a representative sample of the life experiences of the sole subject of this study, an African-American career military woman.

Autoethnography is becoming a useful and powerful tool for researchers and practitioners who deal with human relations in multicultural settings. Benefits of autoethnography lie in three areas: (1) it offers a research method friendly to researchers and readers; (2) it enhances cultural understanding of self and others; and (3) it has a potential to transform self and others toward the cross-cultural coalition building. This inquiry method allows researchers to access easily the primary data source from the beginning because the source is they. In addition, autoethnographers have a holistic and intimate perspective on their "familiar data". This initial familiarity gives researchers an advantage in data collection and in-depth data analysis/interpretation.

This researcher extensively studied this research method for appropriate application to this study's purpose and to avoid potential issues that result in misuse of autoethnography: (1) excessive focus on self in isolation of others; (2) overemphasis on narration rather than analysis and cultural interpretation; (3) exclusive reliance on personal memory and recalling as a data source; (4) negligence of ethical standards regarding others in self-narratives; and (5) inappropriate application of the label "autoethnography". Autoethnographers run the risk of becoming "the target of personal criticism or risk" (Löwenheim, 2010 p. 1029), which Ellis (2004) related as having happened to her. Holt (2003) summarized the criticism of autoethnography as it being "too self-indulgent and narcissistic" (p. 19). Methodologists recognized this as a potential problem, but felt that when one writes about oneself, this does not necessarily mean that the resulting autoethnographic product will be narcissistic. There is a difference between, on the one hand, narcissism and self-indulgence and, on the other, writing about the self.

A major difference in this context relates to the purpose of the writing. Autoethnography is not just about the author's voice. Autoethnography is "a research method that utilizes the researchers' autobiographical data to analyze and interpret their cultural assumptions" (Chang, 2008). Life stories are described as a "part of the way people constitute themselves socially and culturally" (Svensson, 1997 p. 94). In autoethnography the stories are often related through a first-person narrative style that may include dialogue, emotion, and self-consciousness in an effort to understand a section of a life lived in a cultural context.

The writing style of autoethnography can vary, falling somewhere in the continuums between "realist" description and "impressionist" caricature and analytical description and "confessional" self-exposure. This study used a Labovian approach to narrative autoethnography. Classifying and delineating story patterns was a vast field of study, but one of the most influential theories was written in 1972 by sociolinguist William Labov. His research essay "The Transformation of Experience in Narrative Syntax" isolates recurring narrative features in face-to-face storytelling. These features include:

1. Abstract - How does it begin?
2. Orientation - Who/what does it involve, and when/where?
3. Complicating Action - Then what happened?
4. Resolution - What finally happened?
5. Evaluation - So what?
6. Coda - What does it all mean?

The Labovian approach to data collection, processing and analysis design allows the researcher to encode information about the world on a personal level and to produce the final research findings of "realistic tales," "confessional tales," and "impressionist tales" of an African-American career military woman. The cultures and subcultures in this autoethnography were those of the researcher. Those cultures and subcultures included those of gender, race, and the military from the perspective of an African-American career military woman. The research design also provided insight through the final autoethnographic product into how the researcher changed herself as a result of this self-examination. The researcher's own experiences became central in illuminating "the culture under study" (Ellis, 2004, p. 46). The researcher's own experiences within the particular culture of the military allowed for a deeper, more reflexive view of self-other interactions within a broader social reality integrating race, gender, and the military.

Population
American women have participated in defense of this nation in both war and peacetime. Their contributions,

however, have gone largely unrecognized and unrewarded. While women in the United States Armed Forces share a history of discrimination based on gender, black women have faced both race and gender discrimination. Initially barred from official military status, black women persistently pursued their right to serve.

The army has the largest number of Active Duty members (528,070) followed by the Air Force (326,573), the Navy (319,838), and the Marine Corps (195,848). At a total of 1,370,329 DoD Active Duty members, the military force of 2013 is 9.0 percent smaller than it was in 1995 (when there were 1,505,283 Active Duty members). The percentage change in the number of Active Duty members varies by Service branch. Compared to 1995, the Marine Corps has increased 12.2 percent and the Army has increased 4.6 percent. Conversely, the number of Active Duty members is lower in 2013 compared to 1995 for the Navy (-25.6%) and Air Force (-17.6%) (U.S. Census Bureau, 2013).

Gender. Women, who number 203,895, comprise 14.9 percent of the DoD Active Duty force, while 1,166,434 men comprise 85.1 percent of the DoD Active Duty force. Compared to 2000, the percentage of Active Duty officers who are women has increased (from 14.4% in 2000 to 16.4% in 2013), while the percentage of Active Duty enlisted members who are women has decreased (from 14.7% in 2000 to 14.5% in 2013). Overall, the number and ratio of female officers (39,286) to female enlisted members (164,609) is one female officer for every 4.2 female enlisted member, while the number and ratio of male officers (199,587) to male enlisted members (966,856) is one male officer for every 4.8 male enlisted members (International, 2014; U.S. Census Bureau, 2013).

Race/Ethnicity. Less than one-third (30.7%) or 420,340 of Active Duty members identify themselves as a minority (i.e., Black or African-American, Asian, American Indian or Alaska Native, Native Hawaiian or Other Pacific Islander, Multi-racial, or other/unknown). The percentage of Active Duty members who identify themselves as a minority is greater in 2013 than it was in 1995 (from 10.5% of officers and 28.2% of enlisted members in 1995, to 22.4% of officers and 32.4% of enlisted members in 2013). The overall ratio of minority officers (53,487) to minority enlisted personnel (366,853) is one minority officer for every 6.9 minority enlisted personnel. To conform to the latest Office of Management and Budget (OMB) directives, Hispanic is not considered a minority race designation and is analyzed separately as an ethnicity. Overall, 11.6 percent of the DoD Active Duty force is of Hispanic ethnicity (International, 2014; U.S. Census Bureau, 2013).

Participant
The single subject/participant of this narrative was a 46-year old career military African-American woman who at the rank of Sergeant First Class serves at the 185th MP BN (Military police Battalion) in Pittsburgh, California as Vulnerability NCO, Physical Security NCO, Sexual Assault Advocate, Safety NCO, and Equal Employment

Opportunity NCO. The subject lives with her three children in Sacramento, California and simultaneously works at a second career as a Career/Life Coach and Beauty Consultant while also completing her doctoral studies. In order to satisfy the purpose of this research, a number of data collection methods used were common in the autoethnographic methods and which build reflexivity on the collected data: journal records; storytelling of significant people within the researcher's life; autobiographical writing; historical documents, public records, photographs, and video archival data. Data were analyzed by triangulating sources and content; analyzing and interpreting data to decipher the cultural meanings of events, behaviors, and thoughts expressed in the narrative writings.

Data Collection and Processing

The qualitative research practice undertaken in this study required observation, critique, analysis, and synthesis of the situation, settings, and participants in this life narrative of an African-American career military woman. Although ethnographic and autoethnographic reports are presented in the form of personal narratives, this research tradition did more than just tell stories. It provided reports that were scholarly and justifiable interpretations based on multiple sources of evidence. This means autoethnographic accounts do not consist solely of the researcher's opinions but are also supported by other data that can confirm or triangulate those opinions. Methods of collecting data used in this study included participant observation, reflective writing, and gathering documents and artifacts. Of these various methods, participant observation is by far the most characteristic of ethnographic work and the most important for autoethnographers. Because of the value that autoethnography places on the personal experience of the researcher, participant observation is the core practice through which reflections are developed and all other data collection activities are organized. In traditional ethnographic research, gaining permission to become a participant observer in the life, world of those being studied is often a challenge. However, for autoethnographers already fully immersed in the focus situation, issues of accessibility, permissibility, and unobtrusiveness do not present such obstacles.

The primary data collection method in this study was one of a personal narrative. Personal narratives are stories about authors who view themselves as the phenomenon and write evocative narratives specifically focused on their academic, research, and personal lives. The challenge of the primary data collection source in autoethnography–participant observation lied in mastering the art of self-reflection. A system of keeping reflections must be found that suits the nature of the research setting. For this purpose, the researcher collected, over a six-month period, reflections-in-action consisting of handwritten entries, averaging two to four pages each, created twice weekly. These reflections are termed in autoethnography as field texts. Composing field texts helps researchers become aware of the limiting nature of memory and bring details to the "schematic landscape outline." Clandinin and Connelly (2000) agreed that field texts "help fill in the richness, nuance, and complexity of the landscape, returning the reflecting researcher to a richer, more complex, and puzzling landscape than memory alone is likely to construct" (p. 83).

In qualitative research, the step of data collection is not always sequential to or separate from that of data analysis/interpretation. Rather, the data collection process is often intertwined and interactive with data analysis and interpretation. In other words, these activities often take place concurrently or inform each other in a web-like fashion. For example, when this researcher recalled past experiences, they were not in the form of random pieces, harvest bits of personal memories. Rather, the researcher selected past experiences according to the study's purpose of exploring themes that emerged from the autoethnographic narratives of an African-American career military woman in order to gain cultural understanding of the integration of military life, gender, and race. Evaluating certain experiences against the criteria is an analytical and interpretive activity that is already at work during data collection. During this data collection process, the researchers are also able to refine their criteria, which will in turn shape the analysis and interpretation process. The life story interview based on the Labovian approach guided the qualitative autoethnography during the exploration of self-observations and stories. The Labovian approach required the researcher to answer questions, where she was both the interviewee and the interviewer. Secondary data collection methods used were common in the autoethnographic methods and which build reflexivity on the collected data: journal records; storytelling of significant people within the researcher's life; autobiographical writing; historical documents, public records, photographs, and video archival data.

When analyzing and interpreting autoethnographic field texts, autoethnographers need to keep in mind that what makes autoethnography ethnographical is its ethnographic intent of gaining a cultural understanding of self that is intimately connected to others in the society. The cultural meanings of self's thoughts and behaviors—verbal and non-verbal—need to be interpreted in their cultural context. Autoethnographic data analysis and interpretation involves moving back and forth between self and others, zooming in and out of the personal and social realm, and submerging in, and emerging out of data. Like other ethnographic inquiries, this step of research process was methodologically nebulous to describe and instruct because analysis and interpretation require ethnographers' holistic insight, creative mixing of multiple approaches, and patience with uncertainty. Yet some simple strategies—searching for recurring patterns, applying existing theoretical frameworks and compare-contrasting with other autoethnographies—were adopted as a starter in the process of analysis and interpretation.

The author wrote about "epiphanies"—remembered moments perceived to have significantly impacted the trajectory of the subject's life, times of existential crises that forced a person to attend to and analyze lived experience and events after which life does not seem quite the same. Each draft of the narrative clarified meaning, thus refining one's own understandings as if they were new data. The finished product was a text describing the events and situations that occurred in the setting, as well as the underlying cultural beliefs, values, and understandings guiding actions in the setting. The finished product, which answered the study's research questions, reflected the life narrative of an African-American career military woman through the cultural meanings of her life events, behaviors, and thoughts offering insight into the integration of military life, gender, and race.

The researcher used various techniques to facilitate her recall as life story narratives, organized memories, and composed field texts as data. The techniques of data collection included, but were not limited to, (1) using visual tools such as free drawings of significant places, "kinsgrams," (Bates & Fratkin, 2003) and "culture grams" (Chang, 2002); (2) engaging and reflecting on people, artifacts, familial and societal values and proverbs, mentors, cross-cultural experiences, and favorite/disliked activities; (3) chronicling the autoethnographer's educational history, typical day and week, and annual life cycle; (4) reading and responding to other autoethnographies and self-narratives; and (5) collecting other field texts such as stories of significant others, personal journals, field notes, historical documents, public records, photographs, and video archival data.

Data Analysis

The interweaving of data collection, analysis, and interpretation ultimately leads to the production of autoethnography. This means that autobiographical writing cannot come without a methodical process of ethnography and its focus on cultural understanding. However, it does not mean that writing can begin only when analysis/interpretation is completed. Wolcott (2001) suggested that ethnographers begin writing earlier in the ethnographic process, even during the early stage of fieldwork, because writing stimulates, helps organize, and facilitates the subsequent data collection/analysis/interpretation process.

Autoethnographic data analysis and interpretation involves moving back and forth between self, others, submerging in and emerging out of data. Often this requires that the researcher be personal and direct in the area of observation. This process allowed the researcher to operate in a space where she could really discuss the world of the African-American military career woman, not only what her values dictated. The ethnographer will also look for cultural themes with which she will organize the mess of information. Like other ethnographic inquiries, this step of research process is methodologically nebulous to describe and instruct because analysis and interpretation require ethnographers' holistic insight, creative mixing of multiple approaches, and patience with uncertainty. Yet, some simple strategies—searching for recurring patterns, applying existing theoretical frameworks, and compare-contrasting with other autoethnographies—can be adopted as a starter in the process of analysis and interpretation.

Classifying and delineating story patterns is a vast field of study, but one of the most influential theories was written in 1972 by sociolinguist William Labov. His research essay of 1972, "The Transformation of Experience in Narrative Syntax", isolates recurring narrative features in face-to-face storytelling. These features include:
1. Abstract - How does it begin?
2. Orientation - Who/what does it involve, and when/where?
3. Complicating Action - Then what happened?
4. Resolution - What finally happened?
5. Evaluation - So what?
6. Coda - What does it all mean?

The Labovian approach to data collection, processing and analysis design allows the researcher to encode information about the world on a personal level and to produce the final research findings of "realistic tales," "confessional tales," and "impressionist tales" of an African-American career military woman. Coding and associated categorization of data was conducted using NVivo 10 software. The interweaving of data collection, analysis, and interpretation led to the development of autoethnography. This means that autobiographical writing cannot come without a methodical process of ethnography and its focus on cultural understanding. Handwritten field notes began early in the autoethnographic process, even during the early stage of fieldwork, to organize the subsequent data collection, analysis, and interpretation process. The final writing of the autoethnography will begin only when analysis/interpretation is completed.

Writing, Autoethnography, and Rigor in Research
During the qualitative research process, a myriad of concerns could result in a quandary including the gauges used for rigor. Rigor illustrates the agreement of steady structures embraced by qualitative researchers regarding description and predictions of the theory. Rigor is vital for the study's assessment, error identification, effigy and amendment as well as to abnegate the study if necessary. In regard to the intent of this study, the researcher enacted various criteria that united with the theories of intersectionality and the critical race theory to ensure rigor, a dedication to trustworthiness and the validity of the cultural experiences of an African-American career military woman.

The qualitative analytic autoethnography included the illustration of personal culture impressions and other information with the purpose of providing accurate and truthful information. According to Spry (2001), autoethnography must not fall into the realm or confinement of conventional writing. Autoethnography is a theory that is brought forth via a stimulating story that must emotionally engage the reader and it is important that it is not simply a compilation of self-renewal. Traditional writing may not assist readers into transitioning into a motivating place that allows them to look at how their identity maybe developing. It has been noted by Ellis and Bochner (2007) that a study is best viewed as subjective via writing in first person, because it allows the discovery of biases, and writing in third person makes the study appear to be objective. The researcher worked to present cultural experiences that are meaningful and that will engage readers in hopes to provoke social change.

Reliability, validity, transferability, and confirmability. Ellis, Adams, and Bochner (2011) indicated narrator's value context as truth and looked into the reliability, transferability and validity of an autoethnography. Ellis et al. recognized that depending on the style of writing, the topic or one's experiences that a truth could change from person to person. Furthermore, despite the fact the terms transferability, reliability and validity are part of qualitative research they are different for autoethnographers.

Reliability. In this case, another researcher can produce the same resolution as that which the researcher equates to dependability and usability both of which relate to reliability. Researchers clarify a study's scope; define the methods and reasons used to select participants; explain the time required to collect data and the methods used; outline data analysis, presentation of study outcomes and the interpretation of those outcomes; point out the exact system used to build credibility. For autoethnographers, reliability is a system to establish that imagination was not the origin of the story, it could transpire, and the narrator is sharing a personal story. To provide and ensure reliability in this study, merged personal data was synchronized into NVivo 10 software. To determine the applicability and truthfulness of the data the researcher described specific methods used and any possible influences on her as the researcher.

Validity. Validity relates to credibility and encompasses the same concerns as reliability. To build credibility in qualitative research, the researcher analyzed individual transcripts and found a correlation among participants using methods such as reflexivity, interviewing, checking among participants, or peer examination. Ellis et al. (2011) stated that in a qualitative analytic autoethnography, validity encourages readers to believe the story is real, possible, and credible. The reader authorizes the legitimacy of the story, which is done by the story being perceived as useful; it offers ways to make the lives of the author, participants or the readers; and assisting in improving communication between others.

Transferability. Transferability demonstrates the capacity to transfer research methods or results from one group of participants to another, accomplished by furnishing a solid description of a study's limitations and demographics. For autoethnographers, transferability is modernistic; readers examine the story and decide if it shares information about the author or about known experiences. Transferability occurs when the reader can correlate their lives to the life of the autoethnographer's or when the autoethnographer brings light to cultural events that are unfamiliar to readers. During these moments, readers could then see similarities and differences in the author's experiences or by seeing that the story equipped them with a new understanding.

Autoethnographers have created transferability when the readers acquire new information about people and cultures, feel connected to or sympathize with those around them.

Confirmability. According to Barusch, Gringeri, and George (2011), once reliability, validity, and transferability are established, confirmability is achieved. When the researcher develops confirmability, the reader is led to trust in the credibility of the study's applicability and its outcomes. By means of the narrative of sharing cultural experiences based on ethnicity and gender, the research attained confirmability by achieving validity, transferability and reliability of her research. As the autoethnography emerges as a credible story, its purpose is to stimulate the reader's emotional experience, enlarge refection for readers, the narrator and gives a voice to the silent. The researcher establishes validity, transferability and reliability. Additionally, the autoethnography has accomplished its purpose when the narrator is visible within the framework and when the themes echo with readers.

Limitations

Autoethnography is not free from controversy even though it is a significant turn in the history of social science research. Delamont (2007) acutely condemned autoethnography with the allegation that it cannot fight familiarity and the approach of autoethnography is experiential rather than analytical. Autoethnography has several levels that are interdependent with each other, with actions happening based on when the observations are good interpretations are good and result in good information. The hypothesis of the observing stage is important and relevant to think through when critiquing autoethnographic narrative descriptions of experiences and events because it implies that the limitations of the methodology are subjective based on the level of the researcher's observation skills. There is also great interest given to the belief that observers regularly fail to be aware of stimuli that are challenging in some way to the observer. Scholars cite this concern as another weak point of the autoethnographic methodology research design. Other weak points of autoethnography are the incapacity to generalize and the annexation of only one analysis. Several scholars have piloted qualitative research to discover problematic social anomalies calling for reliability and validity criteria to assess collected data. Linder (2011) recognized scholars have the culpability to assure the study is accurate and ethical.

Ethical Assurances

A key issue that remains relevant throughout the ethnography process is the realization that the researcher does not live and work in an isolated existence. The researcher, who is also the key participant, is part of a social network that includes friends and partners, children, grandchildren, extended family, and co-workers. When conducting and writing research, these other lives become involved in the work. Thus, "relational ethics" are heightened for autoethnographers (Ellis, 2007). In using personal experience as data, researchers not only implicate themselves with their work, but others also become a legitimate object of the data analysis, thus making relational ethics more complicated.

The autoethnographer does not regard their social network as impersonal "subjects" only to be mined for data. Consequently, ethical issues affiliated with friendship become an important part of the research process and product. Therefore, the researcher will ensure that all aspects of the research are ethics-led as opposed to method-led. The methodology will emerge in response to the relational activities under investigation as opposed to being described by the researcher.

Chapter 5

Findings

The specific problem is that the life of the African-American career military woman, a member of a marginalized population group, is often dominated by the organizational, social and personal challenges that she will encounter as a woman of color in military culture. Feminist scholars have developed a large amount of literature on women in the military, and they recognize the military is an important site for the socially dominant ideas about gender. However, very little of this work, examines the integration of military life, gender, and race in the daily lives of the African-American woman. The chronic gap in literature on the integration of military life, gender, and race in the daily life of the African-American woman can possibly lead to mentors, counselors, and military policy makers having little insight into the unique daily stressors faced by an African-American woman who has made the military her career profession.

The purpose of this qualitative study was to explore themes that emerge from the autoethnography of an African-American career military woman on the integration of military culture, gender, and race for women of color. Via the life history process, a narrative is constructed so as to make sense of the narration bringing the narrator's meanings and interpretations on what the autoethnographic research design means to a particular study.

In order to satisfy the purpose of this research, an autoethnography method was used. Autoethnography is ethnographic in its methodological orientation and uses the autobiographic materials of the researcher as the primary data emphasizing cultural analysis and interpretation of the researcher's behaviors, thoughts, and experiences in relation to others in society. The life story interview based on the Labovian approach guided the qualitative autoethnography during the exploration of self-observations and stories. The Labovian approach requires the researcher to answer questions, where she is both the interviewee and the interviewer. The secondary data collection methods used common in this autoethnographic study which built reflexivity on the collected data were as follows: journal records; storytelling of significant people within the researcher's life; autobiographical writing; historical documents, public records and photographs. The interweaving of data collection, analysis, and interpretation led to the development of the autoethnography. In order to satisfy the purpose of this research, the researcher's own voice, is part of data collection as a full participant. Given this, the results of the main study are presented in the first person. The data analysis develops themes in terms of influences of intersectional identity during social interactions as well to fit-in and to adjust to a different cultural landscape given the flow of time in a life study.

Data analysis and interpretation. Sources associated with social interaction, gender, race, social influence, and intersectionality theory, informed the data analysis process for the qualitative autoethnography. All names and locations were changed in this qualitative autoethnography to preserve others' confidentiality. The data analysis process included an exploration of the effects of an intersectional identity as a 47-year old African-American career military woman. Intersectionality requires researchers to consider the whole person in the data analysis process, including social categorizations. Intersectionality has different effects on how people perceive an individual and how the individual behaves. Gender, work roles, and race, are categorizations that could intersect through interactions over the span of a lifetime. The analysis of data included self-reflective and personal perceptions. In the case of data analysis, according the goal is the autoethnographer's "situatedness" and the truth as Shank noted (2006). Shank (2006) also noted, "there is no need for standardized methods to analyze data; analyzing data depends on the ethnographer's competence in clarifying data and expressing truth" (p. 262).

Research Question
The research questions were developed to support the central purpose and methodology of the study. The purpose of this qualitative study was to explore themes that emerge from the autoethnographic narratives of an African-American career military woman in order to gain cultural understanding on the integration of military life, gender, and race. The Labovian approach guided the

qualitative autoethnography during the exploration of self-observations and stories. Using the Labovian method, one central research questions is required that will produce the data for the thematic analysis of the study. The following research question aligns with the problem and purpose of the study:

CRQ: What themes that emerge from the autoethnography of an African-American career military woman, offer insight into the integration of military life, gender, and race?

The Labovian approach includes an abstract, an orientation, a complicating action, a result, an evaluation, and a coda. Autoethnographers using the Labovian method provide a summary of the story; answer the questions who, when, and where the story happened; connect story events in chronological order, evaluate or justify sharing the story, provide the result, and go back to the beginning of the narration to tell that the story ended. The Labovian method allows the narrator to identify themes within the context, tells the detailed structure of individual themes through life story narration, allows comparison, and is useful for certain types of qualitative, narrative research studies.

Thematic Analysis of the Textual Data
Classifying and delineating story patterns is a vast field of study, but one of the most influential theories was written in 1972 by sociolinguist William Labov. The Labovian approach to data collection, processing and analysis design allows the researcher to encode information about the world on a personal level and to

produce the final research findings of "realistic tales," "confessional tales," and "impressionist tales" of an African-American career military woman. The cultures and subcultures in this autoethnography are those of the researcher. Those cultures and subcultures include those of gender, race, and the military from the perspective of an African-American career military woman. The research design also provided insight through the final autoethnographic product into which the researcher changed herself as a result of this self-examination.

The researcher's own experiences became central in illuminating, "the culture under study" (Ellis, 2004, p. 46). The researcher's own experiences within the particular culture of the military allows for a deeper, more reflexive view of self-other interactions within a broader social reality integrating race, gender, and the military. The life story interview based on the Labovian approach guided the qualitative autoethnography during the exploration of self-observations and stories. The Labovian approach requires the researcher to answer questions that become the overarching themes of the narrative, where she is both the interviewee and the interviewer.

These guiding questions for developing this autoethnography resulted in the following themes:
1. How does it begin? ***Theme: Abstract from the Life of An African-American Woman***
2. Who/what does it involve, and when/where? ***Theme: Orientation to Military Life***

3. Then what happened? ***Theme: Complicating Action: My Intersectional Identity***
4. What finally happened? ***Theme: Resolution and Life Lessons***
5. So what? ***Theme: Overall Evaluation***
6. What does it all mean? ***Theme: Coda***

Summary
Findings directs its focus on a qualitative study that explores themes that emerge from the autoethnography of an African-American career military woman on the integration of military culture, gender, and race for women of color. Via the life history process, a narrative is constructed so as to make sense of the narration bringing the narrator's meanings and interpretations on what the autoethnographic research design means to a particular study. The specific problem is that the life of the African-American career military woman, a member of a marginalized population group, is often dominated by the organizational, social and personal challenges that she will encounter as a woman of color in military culture. The following section was also written and created to establish the importance of understanding more about how minority military women and the key issues that affect this group and their employment experiences, all with the goal of presenting suggestions that will benefit their lives as they serve their country. For the interconnected nature of social categorizations such as race, class, and gender as they apply to a given individual or group, regarded as creating overlapping in interdependent systems of discrimination or disadvantage this is intersectionality.

Chapter 6

The Autoethnography

1. How did it begin? Theme: Abstract from the Life of an African-American Woman

How does any story begin? It begins with the birth of a child. My birth was one that was unplanned, and I would learn years' latter one that was not wanted. To be clear my mother did make the decision to bring me into this world despite the advice of all those around her. For that I am forever grateful. But the brutal truth is that she was ill prepared to have a child at 17-years old and the decisions that she made would forever be a part of my journey. My mother chose to marry another man before I was born, this would secure the that she would not be a teenage unwed mother. Because this man was violent and would beat my mother it is safe to say that my life began with violence. At the age of twelve I was clear that my mother was of the feeling that my birth had taken her dreams away and that belief would shape how she responded to me. This belief would also shape how she responded to me being sexually assaulted by her boyfriend. This thinking would render me to constantly feel that I would never be safe and no one to change that thought or belief. Forever believing that was not worthy of someone to love me enough to keep me safe or to love me unconditionally. I was angry with God and my mother, for to me they are the ones who chose for me to be and now I was left to figure this mess out on my own. I would not be afforded the hugs, kisses and love that I so desperately wanted and needed from my mother and I learned not to make the effort to get if from her.

By this time, I was ok with the idea that my biological father was not a part of my life. This goes back to the training of being a strong black woman. You will find that the men in your life will most times not be there, and you will be left to fend for yourself. My first lesson in that concept is the fact that my father was not a part of my life as a child. You see my father had left to go into the Army. Yes, in the beginning he did not know that my mother was pregnant, and yes, she married another man before I was born. But all of that is irrelevant to a little girl who is being beat and raped for sport and made to believe that she is not important, simple because of the way she looks. So, I learned survival techniques that the average person would not understand. I never asked why this is happening to me and I never let them see me cry and I never told anyone what was happening to me. Becoming ok with this concept is the foundation of your survival. Nothing surprises you and you are not broken when the men in your life walk away. So, with that understanding I became okay with not having my biological father in my life.

It was also clear that I would be responsible for making sure that my siblings would be taken care of, as my mother would be making up for the time that she lost with being a teen mother and wife. Her weekends were spent hanging out and drinking with her friends. I learned that I would not always be appreciated for the hard work that I would do. This came at the hands of siblings, because they were younger, I was held responsible for what they did or did not do. I was the oldest, so some, how I was supposed to know better. Another lesson learned take responsibility for everything and everyone around you. How could this be my life, a little black girl who no one seemed to love or wanted. Seeing everyone's needs but her own. As it turns out this was another part of my strong black woman training. Everyone else comes before you. Although this part confused me, because everyone around me seemed to be self-indulged. These are the times I cried a lot. Always remembering to never let anyone see me cry. This was also the making of me becoming an angry black woman.

I was the only one of my mother's children to graduate from high school on time and the first to complete college. For me my education was all I had. I knew long ago that my education and things that I learned that no one could take away from me. So, I began to make sure that I had good grades in school. But dark girls were not smart that is what I was lead to believe. This belief was fostered by the behaviors of my mother, her boyfriends, people in my neighborhood and my assigned educators. At any moment my family would remind me that I was black and dumb. I heard it so much I began to believe it. That my teachers had to be making a mistake, there was no way I could have good grades. All the while my teachers on the other side of this picture questioned my integrity. So even though I had good grades, I never really saw myself as smart. I was saddened because the people that were saying these things to me looked like me. They were my mother who was dark skinned, her boyfriend (s) who was dark skinned. More than that they were all African-American. The reality is that I did not expect people of other races to see or accept my greatness so when I was treated unfairly by them I was not broken. Yet, when it came from family and friends it was truly devastating.

"You better leave my daughter the way you found her". Those are the words my grandmother spoke to my father before he left to go into the Army. Well the mere fact that I am writing this autoethnography and you are reading it proves that my father did not leave my mother as he had found her. That is how the journey or life of Camelia began. No plan and one could say that neither of my parents were even wanting or prepared to have children, but as the universe would have it I made my grand entrance on February 18, 1968. By this time my biological father was off living the life of a military man and my mother married to another man who would sign my birth certificate and be presented to the world and me as my father. This arrangement also insured that my mother did not have to give birth to a child out of wedlock.

Even though this marriage saved my mother from the shame of being an unwed teenaged mother, there was a price to pay. My mother's husband was a very mean and abusive man. So, after my sister was born my mother left this man and we found ourselves moving from place to place. This man was later killed by his second wife, because she was tired of being beat by him. By the time I was six years old I could cook, and my mother had purchased a step stool for me so that I could reach the stove and not get burned. My first lessons of being a strong black woman came during those early years. The amazing part to this is that being a strong Black woman even at 6 years old was expected. I remember having to walk to a neighbor's house in the snow carrying my little brother, who was actually an infant and as I stepped over the gate I fell in the snow. Even then I knew that making sure that my brother was safe and did not get hurt when I fell was a priority to my physical safety. For me then it was no big deal, I got up made sure my brother was not hurt and continued over to my neighbor's to use the phone. When I got there, I realized that my neighbor had seen me fall, yet did not come to help me, nor did I get questioned about being out so late with a 6-month old child walking in the snow. I used the phone and walked back home. By the time I was nine I was a pro at taking care of my two sisters and my little brother. There was not time for games or tears, no excuses could be made, and no rest could be taken. During those years I would wonder why I had such a task of taking care of my siblings and my mother was out living her life. On the weekends she would leave to go out with her friends. These trips or outings would usually last the weekend and she would return usually Sunday night or early Monday morning. Every so often I would get up the nerve to ask my mother why I had to take care of my sisters and brother and try to explain to her that it was hard for me. She would reassure me that it was all for my benefit and that the world was not a nice place and as a black girl and specifically a dark black girl I had to be able to hold my own without any help. I soon learned that regardless of your circumstance you must stay focused or die.

Training to become a strong black woman begins as soon as one can walk and by the time you enter kindergarten you are clear on the idea that you must be able to hold your own. Nothing would be easy, and you would have to work a hundred times harder than everyone else. As a little dark-skinned girl, I also had to come to terms with the idea that being the best would not always work in my favor. I learned early on not to depend on others and if by chance someone did assist me I was in their debt. It all started to come together in my pre-teens. I consistently made good grades in school, but in most circles that did not matter. My mother did not take notice and my teachers made it clear that they thought I was cheating. Our community (neighborhood) was small so most knew of my mother and her struggles with alcohol and drugs. It was common knowledge that I was the oldest and that I was charged with assisting with taking care of my brother and sisters. I was also the one that was called to come retrieve my mother from the local bar when she had had too much to drink. So, for most it was impossible for me to be able to maintain my grades while living in the environment that I did. This continued through my middle school and high school years. As it stands today I work to ensure that do not owe anyone anything when it comes to my life and well-being.

It was always clear to me that I was an outsider within my family and community. For example, by the time I was 16 most of my friends had at least 2 children, I on the other hand had non and had no interest in having children so young. Even though I was the oldest child I was the black sheep of my family. My pains seem to be the headline to every joke in my family. I felt like an orange slice that had been shoved into a garlic clove. It was as if the place that I fit in I did not belong. Another thing that was clear was that being dark skinned made me ugly and dumb, this lesson was embedded in me before my pre-teen years. My mother nor her boyfriend(s) were impressed by my good grades or good behavior in school. In reality on most days they would be totally unaware of my presence. So, I would over hear the conversations that they would have about my future and how they really saw me as a person. Most of the conversations consisted of call me extreme derogatory names. I would hear them talk to each other about how I would never amount to anything. I am aware that the reader of this study would probably say that that is horrible, but I knew then as I know now that it was all a part of my training. It would prepare me for the lessons and challenges that I would face as an African-American career military woman.

The pain and frustration of being called "tar baby" or being teased because I had what society deemed as "good" hair which was not supposed to be a part of my physical make up because I was dark skinned. Many days I would cry and wonder why God would allow these things to happen to me. Why did so many dislike me? I began to accept that not only was it bad to be a girl but being black and dark skinned made things even worse. Yet, in the midst of all the teasing and abuse one thing I made very clear to myself. No matter what happened I would be the best and I would be the strongest. No one would have the privilege of breaking me.

Sitting here in American Southwest completing my first deployment after being in the military for over 20 years and wondering how I made it and what is my story about. My story is about a little black girl who refused to be broken by what people told her. She refused to allow that she was constantly told that she would not amount to anything or that she was to not important enough. My story is about taking control of one's life and not allowing others determine my successes. I will say that that all sounds good and it sounds inspiring. The truth is my story is one of pain, abuse, loneliness, struggle and strength.

I refused to let anyone see me cry. Crying was a sign of weakness and as a Black woman weak was not, would not and could not be a part of my vocabulary or my existence. Crying meant that I was buying into the mind bullying of making me believe that I was not unique and special, that the Creator made a mistake in creating me. I remember one of my mother's boyfriend's telling her that I would not amount to anything. He spouted out a laundry list of things that he concluded would be my life. As I listened to him call me a whore, ugly and dumb, I listened as he told my mother that I would live the life of a welfare recipient because I would be the one to give birth to several children of whom I would not know who their fathers were. Amazingly my mother just sat there and listened, and not once did she disagree with what this man said about me. So, crying was not and would not be an option for me. What good would it do? Everyone around me had made it very clear that I was unwanted and that I be nothing more than another black woman with a house full of kids and several baby daddies. Learned then what I did not want to be and that was what they were predicting I would be. I made up in my mind that no matter how many times they called me ugly I would see myself as beautiful. No matter how many times they would violate my body they could not take my mind and my soul. These violations came in the form of sexual assault, physical abuse, spiritual abuse and mental abuse all at the hands of several family members. My story is about a little black girl who refused to die. The little black girl who had to learn to hold herself at night and keep herself safe from the words and actions of the people who wanted to destroy her. My story is about courage and about the will and desire to be more.

What happened to me as an African-American female child and adolescent that caused me to later join the military? Being a dark-skinned girl who was considered pretty for her complexion and had good hair, made for a life of unexplained pain. I grew up in an abusive environment, Friday evenings was the start of the madness. My mother's boyfriend (s) would always find a reason to beat her and my mother would in turn beat me or let me know how my existence made her life difficult. I watched my mother get beat on many occasions by the men who said that they loved her. I knew then that I wanted a different life. I did not want to be a part of this madness. At night I would cry and pray that I would not grow up to be or live the life of my mother. That was my goal. Yet, the problem with this was there was no one who could show me different.

Just before my junior year in high school I moved to Alabama to live with my father's parents. This move was prompted by a string of attempts of trying to live in peace with my family and realizing that it was not going to happen. I was frustrated with not being able to sleep at night worried about who was going to try to rape /violate me at home. Constantly being reminded of my darkness as if it was a bad thing. So, I welcomed the change. I had never met my father and now at 16 I found myself going to live with his parents. I was scared, nervous and excited at the same time. Would this be my saving grace? Would these people offer me the love and safety that I so desperately needed and wanted? Would they be able to fill my love tank so that I would know that I was special? The answer to these all these questions would be a loud NO! I was the bastard child and I was dark, pretty and had long hair, somehow this was to become my Achilles heel, my curse! Although my father's parents allowed and agreed to me coming to live with them, I was instantly made to feel that I was a burden and that I must remember that they are doing me a favor, I accepted the terms. Besides this could not be any worse than what I was experiencing in my mother's house. My grandparents had a daughter my age, so I believed that it was worth the risk. This in itself also added to the challenge of being a dark female child. See, my aunt was a fair skinned female and in the eyes of those around us she was better because of it. Her intentions nor her thought process for doing things was ever questioned. If something went wrong and she was involved it was clearly someone else's fault, ultimately it was mine, the black trouble maker. Everyone was shocked and amazed at how much I looked like my father. They were even more amazed that I was smart and had no children. That seemed to be the theme that surrounded me all my life. I often wondered why I was the one to be picked to carry this label. Was it because of the fact that my mother and my father never had a real long-term relationship with each other, yet they both were in long relationships with their other children's parent. For this I believed that there had to be something wrong with me.

The year that I spent with my grandparents was one of growth and disappointment. This growth and disappointment came in the form of being sexually assaulted by a family member, causing me to realize that my connection with people could never be based on family relationships and somehow, I had to have strength to leave in order to save myself. I was disappointed because when my aunt became pregnant at 17 it was somehow my fault, when the reality was she was pregnant before I even moved in with my grandparents. My growth came in that I learned to depend on only me. No one ever did anything for you because they genuinely loved or cared about you. I learned and accepted that I would always be looked at and viewed as the black girl who no one wanted. I would be the one who was inferior to all because I was dark and a female to boot. This realization caused me to work even harder when it came to my education. Unfortunately, it did not save me from the years of abuse and treatment of inadequacy that was to come. My growth continued in that I realized that I was a great writer, especially poetry. Not only was I good at I loved it. I would spend hours writing and creating a different version of myself and my life through my writings. My classmates would ask me to create poems for their girlfriend's and boyfriend's for birthdays and valentines and many other significant events in their lives. It was simply amazing, people forgot about what I looked like and I found peace and relief in my writings. This is where I continued my strong black woman training.

I would continue to learn while living with my paternal grandparents that I am to be held responsible for those around me along with taking responsibility for my own actions. I would learn how to take criticism for the way I look, spoke, smiled and walked. Trying daily not to be angry. Yet being angry daily. I could not believe that although my location changed nothing changed. Being treated as if everything was my fault and getting not accolades for the things that I knew I did right. Looking at the life I had been given and wondering what I had done wrong. Why was it that I had to endure a life of being insignificant and unloved? Even though I could not see it then, I have to realize that the why of my conditions and experience was that my story would save a life. It would inspire Black women and girls to learn, know and live their worth. They would see that someone else's opinion of you does not determine your worth or dictate your ability to accomplish your goals and live the life you were born to live.

The feeling of sadness and anger consumed me. Wondering how I could get away and leave this pain and frustration that was so much a part of me. I just wanted it to stop. I wanted all the pain, the feelings of not being loved, the feelings of not feeling important or wanted. The more I forgave the people who were supposed to protect me the more I began to feel and believe that I was wasting my time and emotions. The feeling of wasting my time came in the form of realizing I was stuck. I had nowhere to go and no one who truly cared if I stayed or went. A feeling of abandonment consumed me. Forgiving yet not being able to get away from those who hurt me. I began to accept that I was on my own and depending on others only made me weak. I began to release the thought of belonging or being a part of a family. To me family meant pain, lies and abandonment.

I wanted to be a part of a family. A deep desire to belong, to be trusted and believed. When I entered high school, I joined the basketball team, but I quickly learned that you are only popular when you are light skinned and when you are dark skinned your parents need to be of the good financial standing. I had neither so that plan did not work out for me. Feeling broken and unwanted, because the females on the basketball team were just not nice. I would often be thrown a pass when I wasn't looking, which means it was more like playing dodge ball and I was losing. I knew I had to move on to something else when I was accused of stealing another player's shoes and unfortunately all the evidence pointed to that fact. I apologized because it was the only way out and I didn't have the energy to fight. I knew I would probably be remembered as the Black girl who was too poor to get her own game shoes, so she became a theft. The pain of this reality had me crying for days. So, I turned to the chorus; a beautiful voice had I and singing brought me peace and happiness. I finally felt that I had found where I belonged. Singing and bonding with those around me. Feeling as if I finally belonged. It was wonderful to stand next to others and make something as beautiful as music. I did not have to worry about if I was tall enough, light enough, or smart enough. My teacher loved my voice (which was me) and that was all that mattered. My classmates and I loved to sing together. When we were in the chorus room singing all the fear and pain melted away. I felt like I was important, a part of something that was greater than me. I was loved.

2. Who/what does it involve, and when/where?
Theme: Orientation to Military Life
Midway through my senior year I found myself married to a man that promised to help me heal from the pain and disappointment that my life with my immediate family. I was 18 years old and he was 28. I believed and trusted that we were meant to be. It never dawned on me that I had literally chosen the same type of man that I had grew up despising. Before I knew it this man that I loved with all that I knew how to love with was beating me nearly every weekend with no real reason why. He consistently reminded me that without him I was nothing, I would be

nothing. And yet, I stayed. I feel into the belief that if I loved him more, if I did more around the house he would begin to believe that I was of value.

As, I approached graduation I began to think on what I wanted to do with my life and of course all of this had to be discussed with my husband. In the beginning I was reminded that my job and responsibility was to him and building our home. Eventually he agreed to me going to community college. I was really excited because I would be the first of my immediate family to go to college. I believed that my husband would be just as excited, that turned out not to be the case. I found myself being beat not only on the weekends but during the week as well. It never came to me that this was not the way that things should be. I had grown up around this type of behavior and now I was a victim of it. Constantly, being reminded that I was subpar, inferior even, because I was a woman and more so because I was a Black woman who was dark. One day my shades could not cover the bruises around my eyes and the make-up was not helping either, and on this day one of my classmates walked up to me and told me that "if he loved you he would not do this to you". As I tell you this part of my story it is hard to believe my response to him, and it was "you do not understand, he loves me, he did not mean it. I just need to not make him mad".

It was the summer after I graduated from high school, I found myself mentally and physically exhausted and tired of having to continually explain or justify why I was still married to a man who found it necessary to beat me up every weekend. I believed in the concept of marriage and that I could make my marriage work. Then one day my husband came home from work and started an argument. I cannot remember what the argument was about, but I remember the confusion I felt because it wasn't the weekend, so this was something that was out of character. This was something that I was not prepared for this. It was a Tuesday and he had never behaved this way before. Fighting during the week, at this moment it somehow solidified for me that this was my life. I have become the woman that I said I did not want to be. Staying in my marriage and trying to make my marriage work, yet knowing it was not going to work. I had to figure out how to get away, how to be free of this madness. This fight was different from others. It seemed to be more intense and it seemed to last longer I also felt as if I was actually fighting back. The next day came and I was grateful I was alive, and I was in one piece and as I lay in bed my husband had gone to work and I asked for guidance. I asked for a way, to find something that I could do, something that I could put into place so that I could be free. Then, I remembered that I had taken this thing called the ASVAB (it was a test used to assess which military jobs and career field one would be good at) while still in high school. I also remembered that the recruiter had talked about the opportunities that taking this test would give me one day. At that moment, I realized that this was my opportunity to get away from it all to be free from being told that I wasn't good enough. To be free from being treated as if I was not enough and to be free from being told that I was not important and that I did not and could not make a difference. I saw nothing stopping me. I had no children because the man that I loved and whom I called my husband had beat me into two miscarriages, so what did I have to lose at this point? Nothing. At this point I was entering three years of marriage and I was sad because I knew I had made a decision not to put any more effort into my marriage, I was making a decision to save me.

A few months later I dropped out of school and joined the Reserves. I was really excited and surprised that my husband agreed to let me go. But he did, and I was happy. Basic training was tough and rewarding. My eyes were opened to a new way of doing things and seeing myself. I began to realize that I was a lot stronger than I had previously been made to believe. At the end of my basic training I was off to Advanced Individual training (AIT). This is where I was to learn the job that the Army said I was best suited for. I entered AIT in 1989 where I was to be trained as a Tactical Satellite Systems Operator (31Q). Communication's specialist and Cable dog all rolled into one. My company was comprised of about 200 soldiers where only about 2% of the company were females. I was one of three females in my platoon and the only black. This made for a touch learning experience. In 1989 the military world was still not too fond of having women in the military some said that we complicated things. The way I saw it, the men complicated things for us. I was to face yet again someone who would tell me what I could not do and that I did not belong. I did not belong because I was a woman, and a black one to top it off. I was told that we were angry all the time and that as a black woman I had an attitude and I was hard to work with. All of this confused me more than the stuff I heard from my family. I did not even know these people and had not had a chance to work with them. Besides I just completed basic training and had proven that I am strong, fast and able to work well with others. Where were they getting this information, was my question?

AIT was hard. Yet, with each passing week I could feel myself growing stronger and stronger. Even though there were some that believed that I did should not be in the military, I felt like I belonged. I felt as if I had found my new family. All our training incorporated the idea and concept that each of us that wore the uniform were brother and sister's in arm. I believed it and I trusted it. For the first 12 weeks it was perfect. The guys in my platoon began to see me as one of them and even though there were two or three that constantly challenged my ability as it pertained to being a Soldier and doing my job, I took it as mere training. I had learned not to take it too personal, because for me they were brothers, and this was what brothers did. The best part of all of this is my husband was treating me as if I was I meant something to him. Our conversations were generally about what I was learning and how proud he was of me. It was simply amazing.

As we entered into week 13 and the testing of the different skills we had learned began attitudes shifted and everyone began to see each other as competition and not members of the same team. I looked at this as a natural progression. Everyone was beginning to look at where they were going to after being in such a structured environment, it was like they were going through the becoming of age faze. Each believed that they had to prove that they were the best. Quite frankly so did I. We were all reaching our moment of truth. The moment that we proved that we were borne and destined to be soldiers!

As we approached the finale weeks of our training, I began to feel a sense of loss. My brothers and sisters in arms would be moving on to their duty stations and as AIT was ending and I would as have to face the reality of my life at home. One thing was clear I would not be going back to live with my husband. Yet, as I was preparing for yet another transition a week before I was set to leave my training station I was sexually assaulted by one of my brothers in arms. As I laid on the floor, I tried to figure out how this could happen to me. What happened to all the training I had received? I did not scream, nor did I cry, the pain penetrated my soul. I pulled myself together and I picked up the new demon that I would now carry around with me for the rest of my life and my military career. I was changed forever, and I know that I was clear that I must be strong because there was no one who would or could protect me.

When I arrived home from training, I kept to my word. The day after getting back and my husband had gone off to work, I packed my belongings and I went to my grandmother's house. So, in this moment I made the decision to take control of my person and my life. I remember the words of my mother telling me that I had to be strong no matter what happened in my life. That I could only trust me, and I began to accept the fact that no one would protect me like me. I began to pull from my military training to ensure that no one knew what happened to me unless I told them, and I had made up in my mind that I would never tell. It was not easy and my now ex-husband made sure that it was not easy, but I was free of him and moving on with my life. And that was all that mattered.

It was now 1991 and I was 24 years! I was now an NCO (Non-Commissioned Officer) in the Army Reserves and to top it all off I was pregnant with my first child. The fact that I was pregnant was a big shocker for me. Let me explain. The fights that I experienced with my ex-husband were so brutal and physically taxing that I had experienced several miscarriages and the doctors told me that because of scaring I would not be able to have children. So, I did not concern myself with the idea or the possibility of me having children. The discovery of this unplanned pregnancy came about as my unit was preparing to deploy for Desert Storm. Although I could not go, I worked hard with my unit to make sure that the soldiers who would be deploying was well trained and that their families had all the information that we could give them to prepare. I did not allow being pregnant stop me from being a soldier or a good leader.

Time was closing in on the birth of my first born, and I did not want him to grow up in the environment that I did. What I mean is that I did not want my son to grow up around the people who had created a toxic environment for me, because the reality is that my environment did not change I did. So, the things that once controlled me did not control me anymore. How does all this relate to my military career at this moment, although things on the personal side was getting more stable, the fact that intersectionality was still a part of the military and did not seem to be going away, I had to learn to deal in order to be successful.

With the birth of my first child came a new way of thinking and being. I realized that I wanted change and only I could make it. So, when my son reached 6 months old, I packed up my house and sold everything I own, bought a ticket and moved to Georgia. Upon moving to Georgia, I had to transfer over to the National Guard, because there were no reserve units close to the area in which I was now living. The unit that I was now a part of did a nice job of bringing me into the fold. Again, there were not many women and we were all scattered throughout the company, so it was really hard to get to know anyone. But we were creative and me made it work. It was no secret that the culture was that of the 'good ole boy' club. Now, the "good ole boy' club was made up of the white males in the unit. What this equated to is that if you were not a part of this group, you were the last to get training needed for promotions. Your leadership style was never questioned or challenged if you were a part of the 'good ole boy" club. There were many who's goal was to be a part of this group, but there was one that was emphatically clear black women would not and could not be a part of this club!

As I began to navigate through within my new unit, I quickly learned and accepted that in order to be a leader in this Army, I was going to have to work 5 times as hard in order to get ahead and to be taken seriously. There were very few female NCOs and even fewer who were in leadership positions. Which made it even more difficult for one who wanted to advance through the ranks to get the mentoring that one needed. I had to take the advice of my male counterparts and tailor it to my personality. This sometimes resulted in me getting counseled because I was labeled as 'bitchy' because I was assertive and enforced the standard.

By the time 1994 came around I was 26 years old and I had had enough of doing double work and getting nowhere. The feeling of camaraderie was slowly fading. The feeling of family that I had experienced in basic training and AIT seemed to have been so long ago and it was something that many had long forgotten. So, it was with the acceptance of this reality that I decided not to re-enlist. So, in the summer of 1994 I got out of the National Guard and in 1996 I took my Shahada, the Muslim profession of faith ("there is no god but Allah, and Muhammad is the messenger of Allah") and embraced the Islamic way of life. For the next 7 years I lived the life of a civilian Muslim woman with a military background and I struggled to fit in. It was easy for me to get jobs of management level because of my military experience, but again no one wanted a Black woman who was Muslim telling them what and how to do things. I was constantly told that I was too strict, while at the same time being told that I was doing a great job with keep the standards high. I again had to realize that the effect of intersectionality was still a part of my life and would always be because I was an African-American woman. Most days when I went home from work I felt hopeless and powerless, as if no matter how good I was, I would only be told that I was not good enough. So, in 2001 a few months before 9/11 happened I rejoined the National Guard. By this time, I was 33 years old, I was Muslim, and I had a total of three children, 10, 2 and 2 months and no husband in sight. I was working in my destiny of being a strong Black woman. My children's father had decided that the pressures of family life was not for him. For me the desire to get my life together was real. I was a single mother and I missed the comradery of the military. Despite the pain and disappointment, I had experienced nearly 10 years earlier. I was ready to take on the challenge of being a soldier again.

By writing this narrative I know I want my story to be made public because change is overdue. An honest conversation must be had in order for things to change. Sometimes the only way to affect change is to let the skeletons out of the closet or speak to the big pink elephant in the middle of the room. On many occasions the military has been deemed the trendsetter when it came to societal change and yet the effects of intersectionality still exist. Many women are taking their uniforms off at night and are wondering how much longer they can endure being made to feel that they are not enough, even though in some instances they out perform their male counterparts. As I write these passages I realize that my story is important to tell so it will bring to light the challenges that are unique and specific to the African-American career military woman on the integration of military culture, gender, and race for women of color. In doing this it will allow for others to understand and begin to discuss these challenges, which will in turn create an environment that will allow for the African-American career military woman to be seen and treated as a viable part of the military. In telling my story, I believe that women who are affected by indifference and discrimination and the complexity of it all, via intersectionality will benefit the most. In that they will know they are not alone and that they will be encouraged to tell their story in order to affect change. The military and other organizations will benefit in that they will get a real view of the effects of this type of discrimination and in-turn will create an environment where women are treated with the same respect as their white male counter parts. It is my hope that by telling my story it will create change throughout society as a whole.

3. Then what happened? *Theme: Complicating Action: My Intersectional Identity*

On February 21, 2001 I re-entered the National Guard, with the hope of having a better experience the second time around. The unit that I was assigned to was a little bit of a drive from my home and even though my children's father did not want the task of everyday responsibility of having children he and his girlfriend did agree to keep the children the weekends that I had drill and would make arrangements to have them during my two-week training. For that I was thankful. I told myself that we had entered into the Twentieth Century and things had to be different in the military. In all my mental preparation for going back into the military it never occurred to me the impact that my faith would have on how people responded to me. I was prepared for the fight as a woman, and being Black, but nothing prepared me for the fight of being Muslim. It would all come to the forefront in just a few short months after my reentering the National Guard.

I was back in the saddle, attending drill weekends which meant no weekends off because my job counted the weekend that I took for drill as my weekend off. I did not mind, I was a soldier again and I was glad. I was finally comfortable with wearing the hijab (a traditional scarf worn by Muslim women to cover the hair and neck and sometimes the face). I could not wear it in uniform because the regulations do not allow for women in the U.S. Army to wear anything other than issued head gear. For me it was not a big deal because I knew that going in. The first few months back in the guard this did not pose a problem.

On September 9, 2001 there were a series of four coordinated terrorist attacks by the Islamic terrorist group Al-Qaeda on the United States. The attacks consisted of suicide attacks used to target symbolic U.S. landmarks. This incident changed the entire climate of the United States. Our Country was at war again. And no one felt safe. As a soldier I knew that it would come a time I would be called to serve our country in the greatest way. But it never occurred to me with business that it would have or me personally as a Muslim woman. I know it sounds strange considering who our attackers were. But I was so sure that me being a soldier would be the only thing that mattered, there would come a time that, that belief would be proved to be wrong.

As units are being sent to Iraq and Afghanistan and our country is trying to heal from all the madness, those of us who had not made our rotation into the sandbox were still having to make sure that we were trained and ready for war. This meant that we were having a big push on physical fitness, and I remember coming in and wearing my hijab as I had done many times before and the entire drill hall area got quiet. The next thing I knew I was being taken into my 1SG office and being told that my head scarf was a trigger for some of our soldiers who had actually deployed and returned. At that moment I realized that my world had changed and that things for me would never be the same. Things that I had been able to participate in, I could not because some soldiers associated me with the enemy. My heart was broken, and I felt lost, because no one was really interested in how this all affected me as a person or soldier.

As time went on, I did not wear my head covering when I was around other soldiers, and I made sure that I wore more of the traditional African head coverings when I was in civilian clothes. This adjustment separated me from the other Muslim women, because I did not look like the women from the Middle East. As time went on people began to relax around me and realized that I was not the enemy and that soldiering was important to me. But it all reminded me that I was again not being seen as who I was a soldier. So now I had to contend with the challenge of being an African-American, being a woman and being Muslim. There were days I wondered if I wanted to continue this journey. Did I want to continue to be a soldier in an environment where I was already considered subpar because I was a woman and Black, and now I was known as a Muslim woman. Yet, I made the decision to stay, for some this was career suicide, but, I told myself, I would show the world and the Army that I was here to stay, and I would be successful.

In 2004 I became part of the Recruiting and Retention Command in Atlanta Georgia. By this time, I was 36 years old my children were 13, 5 and 2. During this time I was also starting my business as and beauty consultant with Mary Kay, it was always man believed to make sure that always fit more than one stream of income. Having a business outside of the military also allowed me to meet new and different people and also allowed for me to gain a different perspective on the things that I may have been experiencing with my children with life in the military. This transition into the Recruiting command also marked the realization that the military had not changed in its treatment of women, especially African-American women.

During my tenure as a recruiter, my Rookie year I was able to meet and exceed all goals set for me by my chain of command. Yet, meeting these goals and exceeding these goals did not change their perspective of me. I continued to have to face the fact that regardless of what I did or how good I was, would always be met with the fact or idea that I am not as good as the male recruiters. Case in point, even though I hit and exceeded all the requirements to be named rookie of the year my immediate supervisor actually decided to give the award to a male counterpart who actually did not do as well as I did. It was at this point that I decided that I would continue to be proficient in my job but that I would no longer allow it to interfere with my personal life.

This incident also created a fire in me to pick up the pin again. I was reintroduced to the joy and excitement of writing and putting my thoughts, my desires and my fears on paper. This allowed me to become more focused and it also gave me an avenue of release. Outside of running a business as a beauty consultant writing allowed for me to begin to create other avenues of meeting people and a way of creating new relationships. Again, these new relationships served as an outlet of frustration and anger so that one applet and one of my uniform I was still able to be the best recruiter that can be despite the fact that I did not receive the support that I needed to be successful.

2004 also marked the year that my youngest sister and my mother passed away. This significant emotional event in my life also brought to forefront what I believe to be significant in the way that my Command treated me. It was quite heartbreaking in that when my sister passed I was in recruiting school and my Sergeant Major told me that if I left school I would lose my job. This is significant because we had had one of our male recruiters who was in class with me, who was allowed to leave the previous cycle because of a death in the family. I did not argue or cause a scene. I completed recruiting school because I was determined not to be beat and I knew that I was all that my children had, and I was not going to allow for someone to take away my means of creating a better life for them. Six months' later my mother passed, and I was only given one week to go home to make funeral arrangements for her and to get back to work. On top of all of that it took my leadership approximately six months to contact me to make sure that I was functioning properly as a recruiter and as a soldier after experiencing this type of loss.

The reality was I was not functioning well as a recruiter and my numbers began to decline. My leadership did not look at what could actually be causing my productivity to decline instead I began to receive counseling statements for not meeting my recruiting mission. Not only was I receiving counseling statements my leadership also decided that I needed to attend remedial training as a recruiter. My immediate supervisor would also make statements about me having a master's degree, so recruiting should be easy. At this Point I realized that I would not be getting the help that I needed in order to be able to get back to optimal performance level as a recruiter while dealing with the death of two immediate family members. I decided that I would seek help in other places. This included, the behavioral health department on post. After being in recruiting for four years I recognized that it was time for change. I began to look for a new job. That new job took my children and I to Augusta, Georgia.

In 2007, I and was hired into a position as the Readiness NCO at a Regional Support Group unit in the southern part of Georgia. This was also the year that I was accepted into and started my Doctorial program. In making this move I welcomed the change and the challenges that it presented. For most National Guard units, the position of Readiness NCO was considered the most powerful positions within a unit outside of being the commander for the first sergeant. In being hired into this position I became the first African-American woman to hold the position. Even though I was excited and ready to learn a new skill it quickly became evident that many were not happy about having an African-American woman in such a powerful position. On many occasions I would be left out of e-mails that put out information about meetings and taskings that were assigned to my unit.

At this point in my career it became once again evident that I would have to perform 150% better than my male counterparts. That I would always be held to a different and higher standard. As frustrating as this was it became a part of my reality and it also became something that I accepted. In accepting this concept or reality it brought validity to that concept that being a strong black woman. It also gave validity to that old teaching that I will always have to go it alone. But it also brought to the forefront that those who were supposed to be supporting me did not value me as an important part of the team.

I also had to contend with the reality of my country being at war and anytime I mentioned that I needed to go make prayer, I was reminded that provisions for that was dictated by our mission. Simply put, I had to make prayer on my own time, and I could not be late or leave early. Not only that, I was told that I could not really mention or talk about what I needed as a Muslim woman who was a soldier because it was a trigger for some of the soldiers who had been overseas. So now I had become an activating event for some of my soldiers and peers. This fact broke my heart. Even though, I knew and trusted in my heart that these types of behaviors should not be a part of the military, I began to accept things for the way that they were. By the time I was 39 years old, I wholeheartedly accepted the fact that there were certain things that were never going to change and in accepting that I realized that the only thing that could change was me. So, I set out to make sure that I no longer lived my life based only on someone else's personal expectations of me.

4. What finally happened? *Theme: Resolution and Life Lessons*

When I approached the age of 40 years old I began to look at all the things that I had accomplished within the military and within my personal life and I knew that in order for me to be better in all areas I had to take responsibility for my life. I had lived and worked in the space we are I was consistently and constantly devalued as a person and as a contributing factor to the team in the military and had also found myself married to a man who also devalued me as an intricate part of our relationship. I made a conscious decision to continue with my military career. I also decided that I would begin to hone in on those things that I enjoyed the most, my writing, my beauty Consulting business and effecting change where ever I could. In making this decision I decided to move to California in 2010. At this Point I was 43 years old, I had a fairly new marriage and I had two teenage children living at home. This decision also put me in the part time status as it related to military status.

Now that I was part-time with the military it allowed me to have more flexibility and more control of my life as a civilian. Making these changes and realizing that my life was in my hands I began to also focus on what worked best for me and as a woman and a mother. I will admit that this actually created a little riff with some of my peers in the military and it also created complications within my marriage. This became a problem because both sides felt that they should be the ones controlling my life, and I have finally learned how to say no. So in 2012 a few things happened: I got a divorce from my second husband; I began to really focus on my life coaching business, I continued to build my Beauty Consulting business and to also began to really focus on what I needed to do in order to break free from the negative effects of intersectionality as it related to my personal and professional life.

It needs to be clear that the military did not necessarily change, society did not necessarily change, but I changed. I recognized that even though the people around me would work to make me believe that I was insignificant, that I was not a contributing factor and that I was not enough, that I should not and would not dictate how I performed. If I was going to live and operate in this world I would have to make deliberate and calculated decisions. I would have to be ok with being the only African-American woman in the room. I would have to be ok with being labeled a "bitch" or too strict. I had to become ok with being assigned the soldiers who had the greatest amount of personal issues.

I need to let you in on a bit of information. All these changes did not come without a price. Several things happened that tested my will and desire to complete this project. In 2013, I had to take a leave of absence from school because of finances. This was a time of reflection as I began to wonder and rethink the process of completing my DBS studies. Then I remembered that anything worth having is worth working for and I knew in my hearts of hearts that my DBS was worth having. I went to work trying to find a way to make sure that I would be able to take care of my family and pay for classes. Just before my leave of absence from school was up I was offered a Platoon Sergeant position with the Community Based Warrior Transition Unit (CBWTU) that was located in California. This gave me the opportunity to get somethings back in place and get back in school. I was excited and looked forward to working with soldiers who had been wound one way or the other during their military service. Needless to say, I was determined not to allow anything to stop me.

When I took the position with the CBWTU, I was to be there for a minimum of 2 years if not three. Unfortunately, that did not happen. After a year of service, I was told that my packet did not get signed by the Brigade Sergeant Major. Once again, I was experiencing the feeling of being slighted by the military and its leaders. No one seemed to know why he did not sign it. This was really a hard thing to handle, this affected every aspect of my life. Due to this early release I almost had to drop out of school again, because six months after coming off of orders, I was unemployed, my unemployment had run out and my businesses where pretty much nonexistent, because I had dedicated all my time an energy to my military assignment. I had no money, and on top of almost having to drop out of school I was also facing the possibility of my children and I being homeless. All these events tested my perseverance and my resolve not only to make sure that I took the necessary steps to take care of my family but to finish this project! but I persevered, I fought for it and got back in the military and got back on track with my dissertation.

Things became clear once I made a decision that I was not going to allow others to determine my success nor would I allow my circumstances stop me from living out my dreams and accomplishing my goals. Resilience and perseverance in the face of all these challenges over the past couple of years have shown me that I can do anything that I put my mind to. This thinking and way of doing things allowed me to become the most sought out

NCO when it came to doing trainings within the realm of Resilience and Sexual Assault. I was able to write and publish two books in 2014 and start a publishing company to assist writers' in independently publishing their own work. My work also allowed me to be able to help other women work through their own sexual trauma, to tell their stories, to voice their stories, to embrace their stories and to assist them in getting on the path to healing. This all created the revenue that I needed to maintain myself and my family until I deployed in January 2015.

In 2015 I deployed to Cuba. During this deployment I was responsible for 40 soldiers. My additional duties included being the sexual assault advocate, equal opportunity leader and external security platoon sergeant. This deployment would have me away from a family for a little over 12 months. At this time my oldest son was 25, my daughter was 17, my youngest son was 14 and last but not least my beautiful granddaughter was two years old (my oldest sons' child). With everything that I had experienced within the military over the span of 20 years this deployment would bring validity and solidify the need for culture change. The fact that as an African-American woman in a position of leadership I still had to abandon my true self to get things done. Many of my suggestions had to be relayed via one of my male counter parts in order to be heard and implemented.

Once the roster for our deployment to Cuba was complete, I found myself now 47 years old in the position of being the only African-American female within the company in a senior leadership position. The bare facts were that I was the only African-American female in the company altogether. This fact in itself did not concern me simply because that had been the rolled that I had been playing throughout my military career. And I wanted to so badly to believe that things would change. Once again, I was wrong, and I would find myself fighting the same fight in 2015 that I was fighting in 1989.

As the person who was assigned the additional duty of sexual assault advocate, I was responsible for reporting to the commander any actions or behaviors that would compromise the health and welfare of soldiers and the mission. I remember in the beginning stages of our training cycle getting ready for deployment and having to inform the first sergeant about a relationship that was deemed inappropriate for our mission. Even though the relationship did not fall into the realm of sexual assault, but because of the nature of our mission and the regulations that were written and put in place concerning the interactions of male and female soldiers and it was important to make sure that certain issues were addressed before we reached country. It angered me and frustrated me that when I went to talk to him concerning this issue he ignored the information that shared with him. I was also frustrated because the behavior of these two soldiers were also jeopardized the position and career of our commander. I was also angry because the first sergeant did not see the need to address this issue until another male platoon sergeant mentioned how the behavior of the two soldiers were affecting unit morale. I was also exasperated by the idea that I did not know exactly when why he didn't listen to me. Even though I was trained, I was the subject matter expert, and I had been presented to the unit by the commander as the go to person. Was it because I was black, was it because of me being female or was it because I was a black female? This is how intersectionality discrimination works you never really know why he been discriminated against; you just know that you are.

5. So what? *Theme: Overall Evaluation*
I hope to establish the importance of understanding more about how minority military women and the key issues that affect this group and their employment experiences, all with the goal of presenting suggestions that will benefit their lives as they serve their country. For the interconnected nature of social categorizations such as race, class, and gender as they apply to a given individual or group, regarded as creating overlapping in interdependent systems of discrimination or disadvantage this is intersectionality. Example, a woman of color may face sexism in the workplace which is compounded by subtle yet pervasive racism. Considering the limited information regarding military women it is beneficial now to consider research that investigates military life from the African-American woman's viewpoint. Even though I have had some challenges being an African-American woman in the military the opportunities the military offers with education and jobs has actually created a playing field that Black women can play on. Yet is important to level out that playing field.

I posed the question to my children as to what life has been like growing up with me as their mother and what have they learned as a result of that experience. This created a level of fear in me that I cannot describe. This was the time that I would hear how my pain and confusion of being an African-American military career woman has actually affected my children. The next few lines will give you a glimpse into the minds of my children, Jacarah who is 17 and Joseph who is 14. This is how they at this point in their lives view the things that they have experienced as a result of being my children.

Jacarah says, "Living with my mom has been somewhat adventurous. It has had its ups and downs. My mom can be moody at times, but that's been a way for me to learn things about interacting with different people. She has helped me become my best self without forcing anything. Everyday seems to have its own lesson, even my friends agree that my mom is a great teacher and mentor. Not only is she a teach, she is a great friend as well. In some circumstances I would rather spend a day with my mother than with my friends and that says a lot coming from a teenager. My mother makes sure that my brother and I learn and understand independence and that we learn the importance of working for and earning what we have. Finally, she has given me many opportunities that I would not have received without her."

Joseph says, "My mother has a way of recognizing the difference in learning styles. She makes sure that each of us learns life lessons on our own terms so that we will grow into our best self. Living with my mother is simple but it not easy. What I mean by that is that things that happen can be handled but it is not always easy to handle them. In her house she treats people the way they act. So, if you are acting bad in her eyes you are not rewarded with the things other people are given. The thing is, she is always gone and busy, so for me acting bad is coming from her being gone and busy and knowing what she has been through. You know sometimes she is not okay even though she says she is. She does not ask for much; she does not need too. I guess that is where I get it from. I hardly ever ask for anything, some people may say that it is a lie, but when I do I have to work for it, she does not give things away for free, because she wants us to learn independence, independence in that we must be able to take care of ourselves and that nothing in life is free and we have to work for it. I have learned the importance of making sure that my family is safe, I learned that life is a game of chance and that taking risk is a way of learning."

Reliving my story through the auto ethnographic experience has meant a great deal to me and has assisted in my continued growth as an African-American career military woman. This experience has also given me a new-found liberation that I will carry me throughout the rest of my life.

6. What does it all mean? *Theme: Coda*
As I came to the end of this journey I cannot help but to reflect upon how all of these experiences have affected

my community and myself. For me being an African-American career military woman has meant that I have to endure many obstacles. I have learned a plethora of lessons and I have been stretched beyond what I ever thought could be possible. All of this has in turn created a woman who is dependable, supportive, intelligent, humble, compassionate and empathetic to that needs of her community. My community in turn has recognized the value in my presence and the willingness to be a part of growth and change. It has also recognized and appreciated the sacrifices that were made by my children. For without their support, love and understanding I would not have been able to be as successful as I have been as a military career woman.

As I continue to move through this journey of life, and I think about what I want my life to say about me and what I want it to communicate to my children and the young women who are entering the military behind me. I will have to say that the one thing I want to leave for my children and those young women, is that nothing is impossible, that you can accomplish anything that you want, remember the word itself has I'm Possible in it. Their trials, miscommunications, discriminations, frustrations, will all include the ingredients that are needed to propel them toward their greatness. Know that the thought of the glass ceiling is just that, a façade. If you find yourself looking through the glass ceiling, you ask yourself if what is on the other side of that glass is something that you really want. If it isn't, then you step from up under it and create something new. Also, know that if you find yourself in a place where you are trying to decide that the military is not for you think about your whys: Why did you join? Why did you go through all the training? How has being a soldier changed your life? I know my story is lined with a lot of trials and struggles. But it is important for me to note that every test and trial that I have experienced has made me a better soldier, sister, friend, woman, mother, mentor and leader.

This journey of being a career military African-American woman has also brought to light the importance of balance. Balance of home and work along with an understanding of one's faith and the role it plays in one's life. It is going to be important for those African-American women who will come after me to be aware of the challenges that they will face. Making sure that they are able to create and keep in balance within their lives along with making sure that they have a strong spiritual foundation.

Therefore, there must be more responsiveness to the psychological and social needs of the career military African-American woman than in the past. The reality is there needs to be a culture shift within the military and even the African-American culture itself. These two entities made significant impact up on my life as a whole. Those young women who will join the military and who will work in and strive to become leaders will need to understand the importance of this need a balance and the impact that being a career military African-American woman will have on their life.

Finally, how does my story, a single voice, have implications for other African-American career military women? Many of us have turned to the military for employment, education, family benefits, safety, and belonging that mainstream society has not offered us. Yet, make no mistake that we African-American women that enter the military as a career are driven by our desire to serve and honor our country through military service. I hope that my story reinforces that we need for new and innovative military programs that will keep the military an employer of choice for black women. Although some may feel the military's role is only to protect the nation and not to be an instrument of social change, the overconcentration of African- American women in lower skilled support positions is a disservice to these women and the military community as a whole. African-American women disproportionately assigned to these low-level jobs is a barrier preventing them from reaching their full potential. Since black women now represent nearly one-third of all women in the armed forces, there should be a higher percentage of African-American women in top leadership positions across the armed services. The military should work on acquiring the best talent and be more inclusive in promoting African-American women to leadership positions to align with the DOD's Military Equal Opportunity policy.

Chapter 7

Discussion and Implications

The problem is that the life of the African-American career military woman, a member of a marginalized population group, is often dominated by the organizational, social and personal challenges that she will encounter as a woman of color in military culture. New types of questions about women's lives in marginalized population groups need to be addressed within their respective fields of research, including the cross-disciplinary field of gender, race and military science. Studies on organizations, such as the military, present various theoretical and research perspectives to understand differences in "diversity" or marginalized groups. However, the issues that perpetuate and sustain those differences remain under researched.

Scholars indicate that researchers overall tend to avoid the word "diversity" to avoid investigations into prejudice and discrimination of marginalized groups. The purpose of this qualitative study was to explore themes that emerge from the autoethnography of an African-American career military woman on the integration of military culture, gender, and race for women of color. Conducting life history research allows narrators to contribute in setting the agenda for further research in their field of inquiry; in this case military, critical race and feminist literature. Via the life history process, a narrative is constructed so as to make sense of the narration bringing the narrator's meanings and interpretations on what the autoethnographic research design means to a particular study.

Discussion

Limitations. Andrews, Squire, and Tamboukou (2008) also contended some limitations when using the Labovian approach as a method determining the narrative's central and challenging the narrator to maintain distinction between referential and evaluative sections. Although Andrews et al. (2008) presented an experiential approach for a narrative, the Labovian approach seemed appropriate for this qualitative analytic autoethnography because this research study involved comparing my cultural experiences with the larger academic literature on gender and ethnicity. The focus of the experiential approach is not in the event; rather, it provides insights into the personal experience narrative.

Evaluating data analysis. Values associated with culture, social influences, multiple cultures, gender, and race provided information for the data analysis for the qualitative analytic autoethnography. A narrative implies situating different occurrences and events with enough details to make a story understandable. Some fundamental elements of analyzing narrative data include communicating, listening, organizing, and observing the information to detect diverse perceptions. As the narrator of this autoethnography, I was aware that many cultural stereotypes and assumptions exist about cultures. According to Shank (2006), learning how to follow collective perceptions and organizing the events are fundamental elements for a narrative because these elements tell if the information can form a story.

The qualitative analytic autoethnography involved describing information and personal cultural impressions with the intention of providing truthful and accurate information. Aside from autoethnographic methods I also wrote in the first person. Narrative inquiry indicates that people could understand and give a meaning using stories.

According to Willis (2007), writing using first person is the best approach to discover biases that make the study subjective, because writing a story using third person results in a study that appears to be objective. According to Spry (2001), autoethnography must avoid conventional writing. Autoethnography is stimulating story and theory that must engage emotionality to look upon the researcher's identity development. "The researcher and text must make a persuasive argument, tell a good story, be a convincing 'I-witness'" (Spry, 2001, p. 713). I aimed to make my cultural experiences meaningful and engaging to provoke recommendations for future recommendations in the area of military policy and social change.

Rigor in qualitative research. Although several qualitative researchers provided diverse models for rigor, it remains an essential element in qualitative research. Numerous scholars have conducted qualitative research to explore complicated social phenomena requiring validity and reliability criteria to evaluate collected data.

Linder (2011) noted scholars have the accountability to confirm the study is rigorous and ethical. In the process of qualitative research, numerous concerns could result in uncertainty, including criteria for rigor. Rigor represents the agreement of consistent structures accepted by qualitative researchers regarding predictions and descriptions of the theory.

Rigor is essential for the study's evaluation, replication, error identification, and revision, as well as to refute the study if necessary. Some scholars explained the data derived from qualitative study help to understand a difficult and under researched phenomenon. I assimilated these notions in my writing by aligning my story with the theories of intersectionality and critical race theory to ensure rigor, a commitment to trustworthiness, and authenticity related to my cultural experiences compared to the literature on ethnicity, and gender.

Reliability, validity, transferability, and confirmability. In qualitative research, reliability, transferability, and validity are strategies for achieving rigor. Thomas and Magilvy (2011) noted that professionals from different disciplines needed to build practice on the best evidence, with confidence and trust. For a qualitative analytic autoethnography, the rigor process is different. Ellis et al. (2011) inquired into the validity, reliability, and transferability of an autoethnography and indicated narrator's value context as truth. Ellis et al. also recognized that a truth could be different from person to person, depending on the topic, the type of writing, or the experience. Ellis et al. (2011) indicated it is not feasible to remember exactly how the person thought or lived such events and this is an added limitation to the autoethnography method. Specifically, the terms validity, transferability, and reliability, although part of qualitative research, are different for autoethnographers. I followed Ellis et al. (2011) method to meet limitations that may affect the rigor of the study. For autoethnographers, reliability means to demonstrate imagination was not the source of the story, it could happen, and the narrator is sharing a personal story, as I did with my life story interview. In a qualitative autoethnography, Ellis et al. (2011) noted validity stimulates readers to believe the story is real, credible, and possible. Other ways to establish the legitimacy of the story is to perceive its usefulness; I offered ways to improve the lives of other African-American career military women. For autoethnographers, transferability is non-traditional; readers test the story and determine if it shares something about the author or about her cultural and life experiences unknown to the readers in order to provide new learning.

I presented cultural events that might be unfamiliar to readers present and future, where they could see differences and similarities within my narrative. Establishing reliability, validity, and transferability achieves confirmability. To reach confirmability, I achieved reliability, validity, and transferability, through my narrative by sharing my cultural experiences based on my race and gender. An autoethnography is successful when the narrator is visible within the context and when the theme echoes with readers.

Implications of the Study
Because of the extensive personal risk and self-sacrifice involved, joining the military is one of the toughest decisions for a citizen to make. Many African-Americans come from families with a long tradition of service and choose to enlist due to a sense of honor and duty. But unless it can be claimed that African-American women tend to be more patriotic and braver than men, or any other ethnic and racial group, other economic and social factors that add to the greater representation of black women in the military and motivate the decision for many in this cohort to enlist must be examined.

The combination of high incarceration and dropout rates for black males could indicate that they provide a lower eligibility pool for enlistment, contributing to the skewed population toward black female recruits. Compared to black men, black women are much more likely to graduate from high school. In 2001, the national graduation rate of black females was 56.2% contrasting with 42.8% for black males. Though the graduation rate of black females was lower than the national average (by 11.8%), black females were still out-graduating black males by a disquieting 13.4%. An improvement in the national high school graduation rates for black males was indicated by more recent data, to 59% in 2012–13. However, they still trail behind black females. The achievement gap between African-American women and African-American men also extends into higher education. Women, according to a Pew Research analysis of U.S. Census Bureau data, especially Hispanic and African-American women, continue to overtake men in college enrolment.

What is alarmingly high for women of all races is today's gender-wealth gap. But factors of race compound the issues of gender, and black women experience far greater wealth disadvantages than do white women or men of color. As was uncovered by a 2010 report released by the Insight Center for Community and Economic Development, nearly half of all single black and Hispanic women possess zero or negative wealth—double the percentage of their white counterparts (Figure 2)—and black mothers with children of any age have less than 1% of the wealth of white mothers. In contrast, black fathers still fare markedly better than black mothers, possessing 33% as much wealth as white fathers (Table 1). Moreover, black women, on average, inherit less wealth than white women, which indicates that they have fewer opportunities to use that wealth for their children and themselves and to access education, capital for entrepreneurship, and opportunities to build more wealth.

Since couples have the ability to pool resources, income disparities are often mitigated in a two-income household. Many black women are left dealing with severe economic hardship alone, due to the fact that black women are less likely to marry or remain married than white women. Between 1960 and 1985, a dramatic rise in female-headed households occurred, with black women heading more than half of all African-American families by the late 1980s. In 2002, African-American military women were more than twice as likely to be single parents than were white military women (24 percent versus 10 percent). The military has grown, over the past two decades, to reflect a family makeup akin to that of African-American civilian families. Their higher likelihood of being single parents may be a contributing factor to the greater dependency of black women on the military for employment.

The number of black children left in the custody of their grandmothers as childcare assistance, jobs, and educational opportunities dwindle in the civilian sector is another sign that black women enlist when they lack safety nets. The majority of grandmother-led families live in poverty and over half of them are African-American. The exorbitantly high number of young African-American single women and mothers unable to achieve educational training or self-sufficiency through the low-wage labor market and welfare shows that the civilian sector is not offering disadvantaged women what they need to meet their financial responsibilities and goals. High military enlistment appears to be just one of the numerous outgrowths of this lamentable reality.

National recruitment trends have shown for many years that the military is often an enticing option for those who are underprivileged. Taking advantage of this perception, the U.S. Armed Forces have pitched their mass media marketing to the economically disadvantaged. The question that remains is, to what extent does the U.S. military fulfill their guarantees of long-term economic security and greater opportunity for enlisted African-American women? The answer is mixed. The majority of post 9/11 female veterans report feeling that their military experience benefited them in job preparedness as well as in self-development and building self-confidence.

African-American women, who are more likely to be single parents, also reported greater satisfaction with military family benefits. All minorities and women reported having used tuition assistance at higher levels than white men. African-Americans were also more apt than white men to give a high rating to the benefits of housing and neighborhood safety, suggesting that military relocation at the time of enlistment can give refuge from racially segregated inner-city school districts and neighborhoods. Raising concerns about their preparedness for occupations following military service is the fact that African-American women are, however, more heavily concentrated in support and administrative areas of the military rather than technical areas. Though African-American women are now better represented among those holding officer positions than both African-American men and white women, there are still barriers to critical combat experience for those officers seeking top leadership positions in the military.

Even more distressing is the growing number of reported sexual assaults affecting both white and non-white female service members since the Department of

Defense began tracking these statistics in 2006. The Pentagon reported in 2009 that over 2,900 sexual assaults occurred in 2008, a 9% increase from the previous year. Sexual assaults increased to 3,230 the following year, representing an additional 11% rise overall that included a 33% increase in war zones. The numbers continue to rise each year, and in 2014, there were 4,768 reports made by service member victims, representing a 16% increase since 2013. The number of reported sexual assaults does not include those women too afraid to come forward and report them. There have also been a number of noncombat related deaths and alleged suicides of female soldiers, raising suspicions that the Department of Defense has covered up military sexual trauma (MST) in the past. Many families of victims' question whether their daughters' suicides and accidental deaths were actually rapes and murders. It is imperative to note that as the military and the general public develop a greater awareness of this problem, the increasing number of reported sexual assaults may not represent an actual increase in assaults but rather a reporting bias.

Finally, Pew Research found that 42% of post 9/11 veterans have had hardship readjusting to civilian life or have felt they have suffered from posttraumatic stress. According to the U.S. Government Accountability Office, the population of homeless female veterans more than doubled, from 1,380 to 3,328, between fiscal years 2006 and 2010. Many of these women were victims of MST while serving and now suffer from posttraumatic stress and often substance abuse. The unemployment rate among post 9/11 female veterans was 12.4% in 2011, slightly higher than that of male veterans.

Chapter 8

Recommendations and Conclusions

This qualitative analytical autoethnography consisted exclusively of my cultural experiences as an African-American career military woman. I found answers to my research questions concerning the integration of military culture gender, and race for women of color through the lens of intersectionality and critical race theory. For this study, being the researcher and the researched provided the opportunity to think, to consider, and to add valuable elements to the research. My recommendations for future research are to use self-studies, life stories, or autoethnographies, as they are important to understand cultural and personal characteristics of fitting in and adjusting to a different culture in the workplace. The findings of my study also highlight the need for further research exploration of intersectionality during social interactions.

For practice. Based on the findings of this qualitative autoethnography an autoethnographic writing could be a positive tool for practical scholarship bridging the critical gap on teaching intersectionality from ideology to praxis. My recommendation for academics fills the need to identify social locations as race, class, gender, and sexual orientation within a classroom setting, including identifying racism perpetuated by racial and social oppression, and marginalization of women.

Career development. African-American women are drawn to the military due to having few economic opportunities in the civilian labor force and not having a sufficient social safety net. Whether the military productively assists disadvantaged African-American women reach economic and social mobility is unclear, though African-American women in the military often report greater levels of satisfaction in comparison to their peers in the civilian labor force. However, major causes for concern are limited employment options and the lack of psychological and financial support and when they come home from active duty. The U.S. military has an opportunity to be a sincerely "equal opportunity" and "ant-poverty" program for women from disadvantaged backgrounds; with sufficient congressional funding and effective policy changes, it is in a unique position to be a force for positive social change and protect our citizens.

During and before their military service, women of color should be offered special orientation and training programs to work on professional and personal development to boost confidence, self-esteem, and motivation. Workshops on networking, preparing resumes, and other skills pertaining to professional success beyond the military should be offered to those going back into civilian life. Such a program could become a larger alumnae and support network for African-American military women to spur networking all through their military service, and, subsequently, in their civilian careers. It would be hoped that this kind of program, which vows to add to the supply of better skilled workers to the business community, and supports the military, would acquire bipartisan approval and funding.

Sexual assault counseling. Due to increased social awareness that MST is an important issue and negative media publicity, government officials and politicians are making stronger efforts to call awareness to and prevent sexual assault. There has been an increase in resources and funding for counseling and training services. There has been a rise in the reporting of cases of sexual assault as the victims are being given sufficient legal representation and military commanders are being given the tools to combat these crimes. But MST is still underreported, and more can be done to aid in completely eradicating MST from the military. The Pentagon must make sure that the justice system of the military protects men and women who come forward as victims of sexual assault and takes action to prosecute their attackers. A zero-tolerance policy should be instituted throughout the military: if a service member is found guilty of sexual assault, rape, or even particular forms of sexual harassment, she or he will be issued a dishonorable discharge. We must maintain the awareness and pressure on this matter. There should not only be compulsory annual training for counselors and staff officers who handle sexual assault and victims of rape; every single service member should be educated on the consequences for violating a fellow soldier and be required to take a complete course on sexual assault prevention.

Life coaching. Often, African-American military women coming home from service are single mothers with little resources; a lot of these women will likely face hard transitions back into civilian life, grappling with such problems as unemployment, posttraumatic stress, substance abuse, and homelessness. The government should offer programs or work with community non-profits, to aid female veterans in remaining in their own homes, or finding other forms of housing that are convenient, safe, and comfortable, to ensure that these women get the urgent support needed to take care of their children and themselves. Congress should invest in these women and approve funding for continuation of life and coaching, education, and training programs, for at least five years after military service, and for limitless counseling services for military women struggling with post-traumatic stress disorder.

Conclusions
The level on which an African-American career military woman must prove herself as competent and worthy of respect in her professional and personal life is quite different from both her male and female peers and other males. In studies of incivility due to race and gender, African-American women in the military experienced higher levels of incivility than white women, white men, and African-American men. This social inequality can become more distressing due to the stress overload the African-American military woman experiences throughout her daily life activities. She recognizes that the military is a life of choice and that the benefits of this life outweigh any professional or social inequality she

must endure. Yet, in order to be successful as a military career woman, the African-American woman has been called to recognize that she is required to operate in a world with people who at any moment will make it clear to her that she does not belong.

The purpose of this qualitative study was to explore themes that emerge from the autoethnography of an African-American career military woman on the integration of military culture, gender, and race for women of color. Conducting life history research allows narrators to contribute toward setting the agenda for further research in their field of inquiry; in this case military, critical race and feminist literature. Via the life history process, a narrative is constructed so as to make sense of the narration bringing the narrator's meanings and interpretations on what the autoethnographic research design means to a particular study. Examining the daily life of the African-American career military woman through the first-person narrative and emergent themes of autoethnography will contribute valuable insight to the integration of race, gender, and military scholarly literature. The subject of this narrative was a 46-year old career military African-American woman who at the rank of Sergeant First Class serves at the 185th MP BN (Military police Battalion) in Pittsburgh, California as Vulnerability Non-Commissioned Officer (NCO), Physical Security NCO, Sexual Assault Advocate, Safety NCO, and Equal Employment Opportunity NCO. The subject lives with her three children in Sacramento, California and simultaneously works at a second career as a Career/Life Coach and

Beauty Consultant while also completing her doctoral studies.

In order to satisfy the purpose of this research, an autoethnography method was used. Autoethnography is ethnographic in its methodological orientation and uses the autobiographic materials of the researcher as the primary data emphasizing cultural analysis and interpretation of the researcher's behaviors, thoughts, and experiences in relation to others in society. The life story interview based on the Labovian approach guided the qualitative autoethnography during the exploration of self-observations and stories. The Labovian approach requires the researcher to answer questions, where she is both the interviewee and the interviewer. Secondary data collection methods used were common in the autoethnographic methods and which build reflexivity on the collected data: journal records; storytelling of significant people within the researcher's life; autobiographical writing; historical documents, public records, photographs, and video archival data.

Findings direct their focus on a qualitative study that explores themes that emerge from the autoethnography of an African-American career military woman on the integration of military culture, gender, and race for women of color. Via the life history process, a narrative is constructed so as to make sense of the narration bringing the narrator's meanings and interpretations on what the autoethnographic research design means to a particular study. The specific problem is that the life of the African-American career military woman, a member of a marginalized population group, is often dominated by the organizational, social and personal challenges that she will encounter as a woman of color in military culture.

My autoethnography covered the changes and steps that I made as I moved through all the different phases and situations in my life, recognizing that these changes did not come without a price, discussing several things that happened that tested my will and desire to complete this project. For example, in 2013, I had to take a leave of absence from school because of finances. This was a time of reflection as I began to wonder and rethink the process of completing my DBS studies. Then I remembered that anything worth having is worth working for and I knew in my heart of hearts that my DBS was worth having.

Finally, I hope to establish the importance of understanding more about minority military women and the key issues that affect this group and their employment experiences, with the goal of presenting suggestions that will benefit their lives as they serve their country. The interconnected nature of social categorizations such as race, class, and gender as they apply to a given individual or group, creates an overlap in interdependent systems of discrimination or disadvantage. This is intersectionality. As a result, all our struggles will be recognized and will bring to light our disappointments and pain and my story would make a difference, and assist in changing the way women, especially African-American women, are treated within society and within our military.

Bibliography

Andrews, M., Squire, C., & Tamboukou, M. (2008). *Doing narrative research.* Thousand Oaks, CA: Sage. doi:10.4135/9780857024992

Arifeen, S., & Gatrell, C. (2013). A blind spot in organization studies: Gender with ethnicity, nationality and religion. *Gender in Management: An International Journal*, *28*(3), 151–170.

Barusch, A., Gringeri, C., & George, M. (2011). Rigor in qualitative social work research: A review of strategies used in published articles. *Social Work Research*, *35*(1), 11–19.

Bates, D. G., & Fratkin, E. M. (2003). *Cultural anthropology* (3rd ed.). Boston, MA: Pearson.

Bell, D. A. (1995). Who's afraid of critical race theory. *U. Ill. L. Rev.*, 893.

Bochner, A. P. (2005). Surviving autoethnography. In N. K. Denzin (Ed.), *Studies in symbolic interaction* (Vol. 28, pp. 51–58). Bingley, BD: Emerald Group Publishing Limited. doi:10.1016/S0163-2396(04)28008-5

Chang, H. (2002). *Cultural autobiography: Self-reflective practices for multicultural educators.* Paper presented at CCTE Education 2002 Conference. Grand Rapids, MI: Calvin College.

Chang, H. (2008). *Autoethnography as method.* Walnut Creek, CA: Left Coast Press Inc.

Clandinin, D. J., & Connelly, F. M. (2000). *Narrative inquiry: Experience and story in qualitative research.* San Francisco: Jossey-Bass.

Cook, A., & Glass C. (2013). Above the glass ceiling: When are women and racial/ethnic minorities promoted to CEO? *Strategic Management Journal, 35,* 1080–1089.

Delamont S. (2007). Arguments against auto-ethnography. *Qualitative Researcher*, 4, 02–04.

Ellis, C. (2004). *The ethnographic I: A methodological novel about autoethnography.* Walnut Creek, California: AltaMira Press.

Ellis, C. (2007). Telling secrets, revealing lives: Relational ethics in research with intimate others. *Qualitative Inquiry, 13*(1), 3–29.

Ellis, C., & Bochner, A. (2006). Autoethnography, personal narrative, reflexivity: Research as subject. In N. K. Denzin, & Y. S. Lincolns (Eds.), *Hand book of qualitative research* (2nd ed., pp. 733–768). Thousand Oaks, CA: Sage.

Ellis, C., Adams, T. E., & Bochner, A. (2011). Autoethnography: An overview. *Historical Social Research/Historische Sozialforschung, 12*(1), 273–290.

Emerson, K. T., & Murphy, M. C. (2014). Identity threat at work: How social identity threat and situational cues contribute to racial and ethnic disparities in the workplace. *Cultural Diversity and Ethnic Minority Psychology*, 1–13.

Espino, M. M. (2012). Seeking the "Truth" in the stories we tell: The role of critical racial epistemology in higher education research. *The Review of Higher Education, 36*(1), 31–67. doi:10.1353/rhe.2012.0048

Festekjian, A., Tram, S., Murray, C. B., Sy, T., & Huynh, H. P. (2014). I see me the way you see me: The influence of race on interpersonal and intrapersonal leadership perceptions. *Journal of Leadership & Organizational Studies, 21*(1), 102–119.

Garrison-Wade, D. F., Diggs, G. A., Estrada, D., & Galindo, R. (2012). Lift every voice and sing: Faculty of color face the challenges of the tenure track. *The Urban Review, 44*(1), 90–112.

Glass, C., & Cook, A. (2016). Leading at the top: Understanding women's challenges above the glass ceiling. *The Leadership Quarterly, 27*(1), 51–63.

Holt, N. L. (2003). Representation, legitimation, and autoethnography: An autoethnographic writing story.

International Journal of Qualitative Methods, 2(1), 18–28.

Jean-Marie, G., Williams, V. A., & Sherman, S. L. (2009). Black women's leadership experiences: Examining the intersectionality of race and gender. *Advances in Developing Human Resources, 11*(5), 562–581.

Johnson, L. N., & Thomas, K. M. (2012). A similar marginal place in the Academy contextualizing the leadership strategies of Black Women in the United States and South Africa. *Advances in Developing Human Resources, 14*(2), 156–171.

Labov, W. (1972). *Sociolinguistic patterns* (No. 4). Philadelphia, PA: University of Pennsylvania Press.

Labov, William (1982). Speech actions and reactions in personal narrative. In Deborah Tannen (Ed.), *Analyzing discourse: Text and talk* (pp. 219–247). Washington D.C.: Georgetown University Press.

Linder, C. (2011). *Stories of anti-racist White feminist activists: "A conversation with myself"* (Doctoral dissertation). Available from ProQuest Dissertations and Theses database. (UMI No. 3464870)

Livingston, R. W., & Rosette, A. S. (2012). Failure is not an option for Black women: Effects of organizational performance on leaders with single versus dual-subordinate identities. *Journal of Experimental Social Psychology, 48*(5), 1162–1167.

Livingston, R. W., Rosette, A. S., & Washington, E. F. (2012). Can an agentic Black woman get ahead? The impact of race and interpersonal dominance on perceptions of female leaders. *Psychological Science, 23*(4), 354–358.

Löwenheim, O. (2010, October). The "I" in IR: An autoethnographic account. *Review of International Studies, 36*(4), 1023-1045. http://dx.doi.org/10.1017/S0260210510000562

Office of the Assistant Secretary of Defense for Personnel and Readiness, Department of Defense. (2013). *Population representation in the military services* [Annual Report].

Parker, P. S. (2001). African American women executives within dominant culture organizations: (Re)Conceptualizing notions of instrumentality and collaboration. Management Communication Quarterly, 15, 42-82.

Parker, P. S. (2005). *Race, gender, and leadership: Re-envisioning organizational leadership from the perspectives of African-American women executives.* Mahwah, NJ: Lawrence Erlbaum.

Powell, G. N. (2012). Six way of seeing the elephant; the intersection of sex, gender, and leadership. *Gender in Management: An International Journal, 27*(2), 119–141.

Remedios, J. D., & Snyder, S. H. (2015). How women of color detect and respond to multiple forms of prejudice. *Sex Roles*, 1–13.

Rocco, T. S., Bernier, J. D., & Bowman, L. (2014). Critical race theory and human resource development (HRD): Moving race front and center. *Advances in Developing Human Resources*, doi: 10.1177/1523422314544294

Rosser-Mims, D. (2010). Black feminism: An epistemological framework for exploring how race and gender impact black women's leadership development. *Advancing Women in Leadership Journal, 30*(15), 2–10.

Sanchez-Hucles, J. V. & Davis, D. D. (2010). Women and women of color in leadership: Complexity, identity, and intersectionality. *American Psychologist, 65*(3), 171–181.

Shank, G. D. (2006). *Qualitative research: A personal skills approach* (2nd ed.).
Upper Saddle River, NJ: Pearson Merrill Prentice Hall.

Svensson, B. (1997). The power of biography: Criminal policy, prison life, and the formation of criminal identities in the Swedish welfare state. In D. Reed-

Danahay (Ed.), *Auto/Ethnography: Rewriting the self and the social* (pp. 71–106). London, UK: Bloomsbury.

Taylor, S. K. (1988). *A black woman's Civil war memoirs: Reminiscences of my life in camp with the 33rd U. S. Colored Troops late 1st South Carolina volunteers.* (P. W. Romero, Ed.) New York, NY: M. Wiener Publishing.

Turner, C. S., Gonzalez, J. C., & Lau, K. W. (2011). Faculty women of color: The critical nexus of race and gender. *Journal of Diversity in Higher Education, 4*(4), 199–211.

U.S. Bureau of Labor Statistics. (2014). *Current population survey.* Washington, DC.

U.S. Census Bureau. (2013). *Statistical abstract of the United States.* Washington, DC.

Wilton, L. S., Good, J. J., Moss-Racusin, C. A., & Sanchez, D. T. (2014). Communicating more than diversity: The effect of institutional diversity statements on expectations and performance as a function of race and gender. *Cultural Diversity and Ethnic Minority Psychology*, 1-11.

Wolcott, H. F. (2001). *Writing up qualitative research.* Thousand Oaks, CA: Sage.

www.ingramcontent.com/pod-product-compliance
Lightning Source LLC
Chambersburg PA
CBHW070552170426
43201CB00012B/1812